D1173841

ARCO
Literary Critiques

.

Thomas Hardy

Trevor Johnson

New York

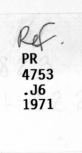

For Margaret

Published 1971 by ARCO PUBLISHING COMPANY, Inc.
219 Park Avenue South, New York, N.Y. 10003

Arco Literary Critiques

Of recent years, the ordinary man who reads for pleasure has been gradually excluded from that great debate in which every intelligent reader of the classics takes part. There are two reasons for this: first, so much criticism floods from the world's presses that no one but a scholar living entirely among books can hope to read it all; and second, the critics and analysts, mostly academics, use a language that only their fellows in the same discipline can understand.

Consequently criticism, which should be as 'inevitable as breathing'—an activity for which we are all qualified—has become the private field of a few warring factions who shout their unintelligible battle cries to each other but make little communication to the common man.

Arco Literary Critiques aims at giving a straightforward account of literature and of writers—straightforward both in content and in language. Critical jargon is as far as possible avoided; any terms that must be used are explained simply; and the constant preoccupation of the authors of the Series is to be lucid.

It is our hope that each book will be easily understood, that it will adequately describe its subject without pretentiousness so that the intelligent reader who wants to know about Donne or Keats or Shakespeare will find enough in it to bring him up to date on critical estimates.

Even those who are well read, we believe, can benefit from a lucid exposition of what they may have taken for granted, and perhaps—dare it be said?—not fully understood.

K. H. G.

Thomas Hardy

Hardy wrote nearly a thousand poems, fourteen novels, four volumes of short stories, a play, a boys' adventure story, and a 500-page dramatic epic, so obviously I have had to be selective. However, all critics agree (and Hardy himself conceded) that his work is uneven. Accordingly, rather than try to give an inevitably sketchy view of them all, I have dealt only with what I consider to be the best of his novels and poems. I have contented myself with a note on *The Dynasts*, thinking it better to leave it alone than venture a superficial comment on what is a vast and, to be truthful, a not very approachable achievement. With one or two exceptions, the short stories are less successful than the novels, and these, too, I have dealt with very briefly. It remains only to stress that there is very little in Hardy's work which is totally unrewarding, and I hope this study may persuade readers to a further exploration of a great writer's work, and in particular tempt those who may only know the novels to look at the poems, which are still too seldom read. I naturally owe a considerable debt to other writers on Hardy, more particularly where the novels are concerned, which I take this opportunity of acknowledging.

H. A. T. J.

Contents

1. Hardy's Life   *page* 9

2. His Readers   23

3. The Poetry   29

4. The Novels   88

5. Notes on *The Dynasts* and the Short Stories   153

   Reading List   155

   Index   158

The Author

Trevor Johnson, M.A. (Oxon.), is Principal Lecturer and Head of the English Department at Mather College of Education, Manchester.

Hardy, aged 53, by William Strang. This etching shows Hardy's 'rough, masculine, persuasive force'.

Aug 19 – Went to sketch at Boscastle Harbour.

Searching for the glass (water colour sketching in valley)

E.L.G. by T.H. Aug 19 1870

Hardy's sketch of Emma searching for a lost wine-glass. This drawing may well have inspired the poem *Under the Waterfall* 43 years later.

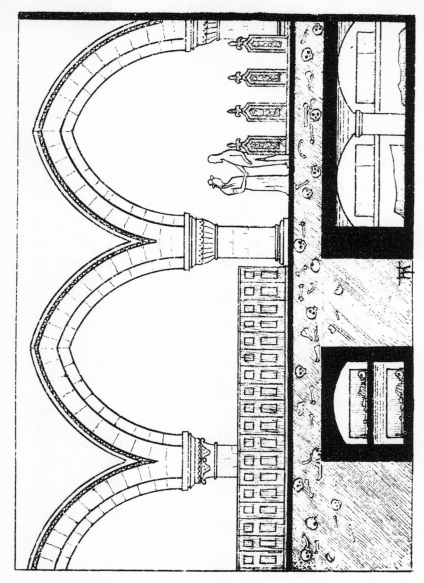

Hardy's drawing to illustrate his poem *Her Dilemma* (1866). He was not a great artist but he conveys the macabre quality of the poem effectively.

I

Hardy's Life

If, when hearing that I have been stilled at last, they stand by the
   door,
   Watching the full-starred heavens that Winter sees,
   Will this thought rise on those who will meet my face no more,
   He was one who had an eye for such mysteries?

AFTERWARDS

The two most obvious facts about Thomas Hardy's life are its
length and uneventfulness. To say that he lived to be eighty-
eight is in itself not specially impressive. But when Hardy was
born in 1840 at the village of Upper Bockhampton, near
Dorchester, Queen Victoria—then just about to marry Prince
Albert—had only reigned three years. How many would have
guessed that this frail child of a country stonemason would see
the Queen's grandson on the throne for seventeen years? But
he did, and when he died in 1928 he had also seen the ponderous
façade of Victorian England first crack under the strain of the
Boer War and the political upheavals of Edward VII's reign,
then crumble into ruin under the impact of the First World War
and the vast changes it brought in its wake. One generation
before Hardy's birth had come Napoleon's conquests and
England's lonely defiance, which he was to record on the vast
canvas of *The Dynasts*; one generation after his death the Second
World War began and the world Hardy had known was lost to
sight for ever.

When this small, spry, seemingly indestructible old man died
as, with pardonable pride, he was about to issue a new volume
of poems on his eighty-eighth birthday, T. S. Eliot's *Waste Land*
had been on sale for six years. His first successful novel, *Under the*

9

Greenwood Tree, came out in 1873—the year Tennyson's poems were first collected. His last book was aptly entitled *Winter Words*, and one of the poems tells us a great deal about Hardy's own view of life. The first verse runs:

> I am the one whom ring-doves see
>> Through chinks in boughs,
>> When they do not rouse
>> In sudden dread
> But stay on cooing, as if they said,
>> 'Oh; it's only he'.

and it was as an observer, quiet, sharp-eyed and detached, that Hardy liked to see himself; one who pondered on life and its 'mysteries', as he puts it in more than one poem. This detachment was necessary, he thought, to come at the truth about life, a truth to be proclaimed when found, however unpleasant. For honesty, with himself and others, was the most marked feature of his character. In his haunting, gentle poem, *To an Unborn Pauper Child*, Hardy declares a deep longing to help one so handicapped even before birth, but, he says:

> . . . I am weak as thou and bare.
> No man may change the common lot to rare.

and his steadfast refusal to distort his work into mere topical propaganda, forgotten within weeks, goes far to account for a life in which, as one of his biographers says, 'nothing seems to have happened'. Indeed, as with William Shakespeare, the important facts of Hardy's life could be written handily on a postcard. He only wrote his autobiography after a lot of urging, and then put it into the third person so that it was eventually published after his death as his second wife's work, though in reality only the last few chapters were hers.

It would then be pointless to deal with Hardy's life year by year, and I shall not try to do so. Instead I shall attempt some sketches of various periods of his life, with occasional glances backwards and forwards. We must go to *The Life of Thomas Hardy* (Macmillan, 1962), supposedly written by Mrs. F. E. Hardy, for a great deal of fascinating material about him, though some important matters are glossed over or left out, as was natural for an old man looking backwards at what it pained him to recall. (Where quotations follow they are taken from this source unless otherwise indicated.)

'THE SELF UNSEEING', 1840–56

Impressions made in childhood are generally indelible, and this is a truth of vital importance for an understanding of Hardy, whose early years were the seed-bed of his later creative flowering. Hardy was the third successive Thomas in a family which came from the same stock as Nelson's flag-captain. His mother's maiden name was Jemima Hand. She lost her father as a child, and knew real poverty. Even so, Hardy tells us, 'she read every book she could lay hands on', and grew up to be a woman of ability, judgment, and 'an energy that might have carried her to incalculable issues'. As a very old lady indeed she walked over several miles of icy road to see her son in his home, and when he asked her why she had done so, replied, 'To enjoy the beauties of nature, of course, and why shouldn't I?' One might think that she would have been the dominant influence on Hardy as a child, but his father was a man of character too, even if he didn't 'possess the art of enriching himself by business', as Hardy drily puts it. Thomas Hardy senior was a fine craftsman; but more deeply rooted even than his pride in workmanship was his love of music. This passionate attachment he communicated to his son, who was a child 'of ecstatic temperament, extraordinarily sensitive to music'. Though Hardy's father may not have been enterprising, the family were never really poor, and Hardy's was an unusually happy childhood, about which he tells us all we need to know in a tiny lyric of extraordinary beauty and lucidity, which deserves quotation:

> She sat here in her chair,
> Smiling into the fire;
> He who played stood there,
> Bowing it higher and higher.

Childlike, I danced in a dream;
Blessings emblazoned that day;
Everything glowed with a gleam;
Yet we were looking away!

THE SELF UNSEEING

So clear is the picture, so unerringly selective are Hardy's powers
of seeing and saying, it is as if a small window in time were
opened for us, and Hardy clearly suggests by his title—*The Self
Unseeing*—the kind of timeless and self-absorbed delight that
only children know. He quickly learned to do more than
listen to music. He mastered the violin when quite small, and
could soon play hundreds of tunes—both the fine four-square
melodies of the hymns he sang in Stinsford church every
Sunday, and the airs, ancient and beautiful, grave and gay,
mocking and sorrowful, of the old ballads and folk-songs like
the one Joseph Poorgrass quavers out in *Far from the Madding
Crowd*:

I sowed the seeds of love.
It was all in the Spring—

which, oddly enough, was the very first song to be collected
by Cecil Sharp and set him off on a life's work. Hardy had noted
it long before, and it is very old indeed. The story of poor Fanny
Robin in the novel where it occurs is mirrored in the theme of
the ballad, just as the song Bathsheba Everdene sings in the
same book foretells her misfortune. It is hard to overestimate
the influence of this oral literary tradition in Hardy, and some
knowledge of folk-song is very helpful in an appreciation of his
poems. In terms of subject and treatment the debt is very
large, and his taste for (generally dismal) versified anecdotes—
a weakness of his verse—probably derives also from the later,
and feebler, 'broadsheet' ballads.

As one would expect, Hardy early became an avid reader,
able to spell out the titles of *The Cries of London*—a large picture-
book—at three. He also displayed remarkable powers of
memory, which he never lost: dressing up as a 'parson' in the
table-cloth, he delivered sermons which were 'a patchwork of

[remembered] sentences used by the vicar'. He remarks (with that gentle humour of his which often goes unnoticed) that people thought he would have to become a parson, 'being obviously unfit for any practical pursuit'.

Later he did well at the village school and caught the eye of Mrs. Julia Martin, the squire's wife, who had founded it. Whatever she saw in him—perhaps just a 'star' pupil—his feeling for her was intense, 'almost that of a lover', he says. Accordingly, when his parents fell out with Mrs. Martin over his move to a school in Dorchester, the sensitive child received a stinging foretaste of the pain and humiliation that could be caused by the elaborate and rigid Victorian class structure. He never forgot this, and his first, unpublished, novel, *The Poor Man and the Lady*, was an impassioned outcry against a system in which accident of birth conferred vast advantages and erected a thorny hedge of snobbery and formality between people otherwise meant for friendship and love.

Hardy's new schoolmaster, Mr. Isaac Last, was clearly a very able teacher. At fourteen Hardy was proficient at Latin, reading it with considerable fluency; he knew Shakespeare, the Bible and *Pilgrim's Progress* thoroughly. Fielding's robust humanity and the romantic historical novels of Scott and Dumas both delighted him, and he also reached a passable standard in French. Perceptive and sympathetic as he was, literature made a deep impression on him, and, as Evelyn Hardy has pointed out, he had already begun his life-long habit of marking passages in books, some of which foreshadow the darker preoccupations of later novels. Although rather shy and withdrawn, disliking to be touched and enjoying solitude, he was much in demand as a fiddler at local dances.

The world Hardy then lived in was unimaginably fiercer than ours. He saw two public executions, and heard tales from his father of rick-burnings, and of savage punishments, some grossly unjust, used in reprisal. Extreme poverty was everywhere to be seen, and the callous Poor Law system accelerated the drift of proud and skilled, but workless, men to the big towns. Hardy's childhood was passed in a period when agriculture was at a low ebb. My own grandfather, born only three years after Hardy, wrote down the story of his journey to London in ballad form. He was a carter, but could not get work after much wandering in Wiltshire and Dorset, so, as he says:

> I then grew tired of wandering
> But yet too stubborn to bend—

and set off to work his way, sleeping in barns, washing in rivers, and pawning odds and ends, to the 'big city', as he calls it. There he worked on the railway and elsewhere, but only casually; often he was reduced to a kind of begging:

> I remember going through Chelsea
> A-singing with other men,
> Folks throwed us out some coppers
> From a window now and then.

This was a bitter experience; he was an intelligent man proud of his skill; and it was all too typical. Hardy must have seen this clash of an ancient way of life with a newer, more ruthless one, and he makes it a major element in much of his writing. It was the first experience perhaps to set up in that quick, impressionable mind a sense both of 'man's inhumanity to man' and of the cruel inevitability of changes which were no man's fault. Nevertheless up to the age of sixteen Hardy was 'still a child', as he tells us, and one feels these years were his most cloudless. As the Jacobean dramatist Tourneur (whose own plays were more sombre than Hardy's darkest work) wrote:

> . . . Joye's a subtle elf
> I think man's happiest when he forgets himself.

—an enviable state, and one that Hardy was seldom to achieve again.

'THE SUN ON THE BOOKCASE', 1856-71

This is the title of a poem in which Hardy pictures a student who is reminded by the sun reddening his books that he has 'wasted' a whole day in dreaming of romance and great achievement. The 'student' is almost certainly Hardy, who during this period was studying, nominally architecture, but in reality life, art and writing in the widest sense. It was a time of promise, achievement, and vast hopes—he called it 'the buoyant time' in fact—but also one increasingly clouded by doubts about the truth of the religious beliefs in which he had been brought up and which he had accepted without question.

There is not much doubt that Hardy could have worked his way to a university, but his father hadn't the money to keep him at school. So Hardy was apprenticed to John Hicks, a local architect who had been impressed with the boy's intelligence and had asked for him as a pupil. In Hicks's Dorchester office Hardy met three young men, all older than he. They argued incessantly, especially about religion, and Hardy promptly began to learn Greek so as not to be outdone by them in commenting on the New Testament. They must have done some work at times as Hardy became a first-class draughtsman, but Hicks liked books himself and was an easy-going master. In these good-humoured, argumentative surroundings Hardy was in his element, and, as he says, 'Like a conjurer at the fair, [I kept] in the air the three balls of architecture, scholarship and dance-fiddling', for he slept at home, and still, so to speak, kept one foot in the country.

Next door, at his school, was William Barnes—a university in himself—scholar, folklorist, linguist and poet. Day by day Hardy taxed the older man with questions of all kinds; week by week he read Barnes's dialect poems as they appeared in the local paper. They were very good poems too, though Hardy did not make much use of dialect in his own poetry, probably realising that it would only appeal to limited audiences.

At twenty-three Hardy had finished his training and found work in London with Arthur Blomfield, then the coming young man of English architecture and in the vanguard of those 'Gothic Revivalists' who were about to flood England with insipid imitations of the masterworks of the Middle Ages. Most of Hardy's work was concerned with church restoration, which in practice often meant destruction and uglification. I think it is likely that Hardy, who later regretted his share in this, reinforced an already powerful dislike of all things shoddy and gimcrack, eye-catching and cheap, and learned particularly to detest ornament 'applied' to work instead of springing naturally out of it. This would help to account for his deliberate rejection of 'elegance' and 'polish' in his novels and poems. For by this time he had begun to write, winning two architectural essay prizes, though failing to get his poems published.

It was Dr. Johnson who said 'the man who is tired of London is tired of life'. Hardy did not need convincing of this. He fought his way into Phelps's excellent and cheap Shakespeare productions. There was a wealth of music, operas and oratorios to listen to. (Blomfield even formed an office choir in which Hardy sang bass.) Hardy had the eye of a painter, if not the hand; now he lost himself in the vision of the Old Masters—so much so that he later came to lard his novels with references to them, often hauling them in haphazard to the detriment of the narrative, but always impelled by his admiration of their 'truth to life'. The city was for Hardy 'crowded with culture', and the reference reminds us that he admired Browning most of all the poets then famous. What is important, though, what really makes this a crucial point in Hardy's life, is his growing conviction that the idea of a world under benevolent supernatural direction could not be squared with the facts of life as he saw them—a conviction expressed in his earliest poems. Not long before this he had thought of going to Cambridge, being ordained, and becoming a village curate. Fortunately, after some reading of theology, which could not have mixed well with his excursions into Darwin's *Origin of the Species* (a book then thought positively wicked because it cast doubt on the literal truth of the Bible), he let the idea 'drift out of sight'.

Chance took a hand in Hardy's own life now. Illness, London's stuffy air and his own 'dislike for life as a science of climbing' sent him back to live at home and work for Hicks. From this decision to pursue a life of peace and quiet endeavour, flowed his first passionate and tragic love affair, his second romance and marriage, his career as a novelist and much of his best poetry. While he was staying at his own home in the summer of 1867 he met Tryphena Sparks, the sixteen-year-old daughter of a family related to his own, and living in Puddletown, within easy walking distance of Upper Bockhampton. He fell in love with her—something which no one who has seen her portrait (taken when she was eighteen) will find in the least surprising—for she was, with her sloe-black hair, dark eyes and finely-boned face, indubitably beautiful. She was intelligent too, passing out as a teacher, fifth in the lists, at Stockwell Training College in 1869. Hardy must have been starved of informed conversation after leaving London. No one could read the poems without realising that Hardy's was an ardent nature, and so it seems was hers. Theirs was a passionate, tempestuous and, one suspects, precarious relationship. It appears highly probable that Tryphena bore Hardy a child in 1868—a matter which was, of course, concealed, though the child was well cared for in later years. At all events, Tryphena returned Hardy's engagement ring in 1872, after five years—an agonising blow for him. She died, having married and had children, in 1890, and Hardy wrote a poem addressed to her in which he calls her 'my lost prize'. Her influence on his work is incalculable. Certainly she appears as Sue in *Jude*, several poems refer to her, and it would be foolish to ignore the fact that Hardy's whole life was affected by this long love-affair in various ways. The book which reveals these long-hidden facts (*Providence and Mr. Hardy*, by Lois Deacon and Terry Coleman) places beyond doubt Hardy's own bitter knowledge that, as one of his finest poems puts it:

The paths of love are rougher
Than thoroughfares of stones.

While all this was going on, Hicks's leisured business gave Hardy time to write what he later called 'a striking socialistic novel'. I have mentioned this already, and *The Poor Man and the Lady* drew the attention of Alexander Macmillan, to whom Hardy sent it. The publisher wrote a long letter in which he praised its 'promise', but disliked the scathing criticism of wealthy society, which he thought 'excessive'.

Hardy tried another publisher, and so met Chapman & Hall's

reader, the poet and novelist, George Meredith, who gave Hardy sensible advice but also sent him down a blind alley, that of the melodramatic novel with a tangled, complex skein of coincidences for a plot. *Desperate Remedies* it was called, and we can afford to leave one of its characters the last word: 'Here's a rum story,' he says.

'SWEEPING LIKE SUMMERTIDE WIND ON OUR WAYS', 1870–85

The threatened collapse of an old Cornish church took Hardy to St. Juliot on 7 March 1870, a date he never forgot. Much later he summoned the whole complex of emotion and recollection up again and put it into his gayest, most lilting poem, *When I set out for Lyonnesse*. What happened, like any other love story, is soon told. He met, at the rectory where he stayed, Emma Lavinia Gifford, the rector's sister-in-law. She was a little younger than Hardy, attractive, and no doubt ready to welcome a stranger to what was then an unknown part of Cornwall. They walked together in the strangely beautiful countryside. Inevitably, one feels, they fell half in love, and though nothing was said directly, as they walked in the garden after Hardy had announced his departure, a delicate hint was given and taken:

> Even then the scale might have turned
>   Against love by a feather,
> But crimson one cheek of hers burned
>   As we came in together.

As with all Hardy's work on this theme, we are conscious of the precarious nature of love. But the 'scale' dropped towards him, and after many other visits to St. Juliot—few churches can have had such close architectural supervision—they married in 1874.

In the meantime *Under the Greenwood Tree*, where Hardy found his true bent, had appeared in 1872 and had considerable critical though little financial success. The publication of *Far from the Madding Crowd*—an unquestioned masterpiece—enabled Hardy to marry in some security. Even so his wife and he wandered about Europe and England 'like tramps', with nothing but boxes of books and a bookcase besides their clothes, and, as a sole concession to domesticity, a door-scraper! At length they settled at Sturminster Newton, in a villa with a wide vista of water-meadows, and in this serene and lovely setting they lived out a two-year idyll amid a profusion of bird-song and garden fruit in summer, and surrounded by floods in winter. However, Hardy decided to return to London in 1878, after *The Return of the Native* had been published. Years later he looked back at his journal where he had written 'End of Sturminster Newton Idyll', and added sadly, 'our happiest time'. He and his wife had wanted children but none came, and now they entered London society after their 'high expectant hearts' had met with disappointment. The summertide wind of the idyll had changed direction, and perhaps it isn't too fanciful to hear in the spiritual north-easter that howls through some pages of *The Return of the Native* an echo of Hardy's own unrest.

'TURMOILED YEARS OF BELLIGERENT FIRE', 1878–1912

This line refers to the First World War, yet it is hardly less applicable to Hardy himself in this his greatest creative period. No longer young, he was possessed with a driving energy and nothing seemed too much for him. He wrote nine more novels, three volumes of short stories, published three collections of poems, and completed the most massive, unique and characteristic achievement of his life, the 520 pages of mingled prose, dramatic, lyric and philosophic verse which he called *The Dynasts*—a god's-eye view of the Napoleonic Wars. He came gradually to be acknowledged, not without rancour and dispute, as the greatest English writer of his time, he received a well-deserved Order of Merit, honorary Doctorates were awarded by the universities, and nosy visitors pestered him in his new house, 'Max Gate', near Dorchester, where he lived for the rest of his life when not in London.

Outwardly he seemed to live a tranquil and successful life. But there was a pattern of storm beneath the peaceful surface, and William Strang's portrait of him (see illustrations) is in striking contrast to the dignified old man who appears on the cover of this book. There is an air of turbulence, perhaps of a passionate nature foiled, a sanguine temperament chilled, in this fine etching, or so it seems to me. The truth is that, during these three decades of stormy creation, critical praise and derision, culminating in widespread public acclaim, Hardy's private life was overshadowed by what at length became his wife's virtual insanity. There isn't any real doubt that in her later years she was a victim of delusions, among them the conviction that she had married much beneath her, and that she herself had actually written, or anyway suggested, much of Hardy's work. (Of course she had *copied* a good deal for him.) Her public behaviour to her husband became insulting, and, what must have been exquisitely painful to Hardy, who was always thin-skinned anyway, she openly prided herself more upon being an archdeacon's niece than upon being married to the greatest living English writer. Hardy was modest enough but he had his pride. His wife even endeavoured to stop publication of *Jude*, which she thought 'immoral'. In face of all the evidence she asserted that Hardy was really an orthodox Christian, and in her last years she produced several books of mystical gobbledygook. In her, until recently unpublished, *Recollections* Hardy cut out one supremely snobbish remark himself, when he read the manuscript after her death, though no one else was likely to see it.

All this is painful, but not I hope unprofitable. It is important to realise that Hardy suffered a great deal, because otherwise his own attitude to life might seem unreasoning. But he did idealise his wife, and he had been spellbound in Cornwall. Now Hardy, who was heroically loyal to his wife, discovered the agonising truth W. B. Yeats expressed in:

> Maybe the bride-bed brings despair
> For each an imagined image brings
> And finds a real image there . . .

He didn't repine or try to get rid of her but the scars are to be seen in his work. To a nature gentle, self-deprecating, and withal desperately sensitive, work was perhaps in part an escape from, in part a compensation for, love, the 'sum of human delight', as he once called it.

Mrs. Hardy died, unexpectedly, in 1912. Though Hardy was with her at the last, she never regained consciousness after a disagreement that, by an unlucky chance, had occurred earlier. Unjustified remorse and grief long held in check now broke, to release a clear stream of the most moving love poems of this or of any other century, recapturing (as if Time had never cracked it with his cold finger) that crystal world of joy and desire which the lovers had inhabited in their first years together. These poems close an epoch in Hardy's life as surely as if a great door had swung to.

'NAY RUSH NOT, TIME SERVES, WE ARE GOING', 1912–28

This was in many ways a happier phase in Hardy's life than the previous one. In 1914 he married Florence Emily Dugdale, a charming and sympathetic woman much younger than he, and with her his home-life, which had dissolved into muddle and interference from sightseers, became calm and ordered. There was never anything doddery about Hardy. He wrote more lyrical poetry and worked on his 'memoirs'. His home became a place of pilgrimage for young writers like Edmund Blunden, Robert Graves, T. E. Lawrence and Siegfried Sassoon. This pleased him, and like Dr. Johnson he 'kept his friendships in good repair', still going about the countryside a good deal. He liked to tell stories about himself: one of the best is the tale of how, when cycling, he skidded on the wet streets and fell in the mud. A man came to his rescue and kindly helped to wipe him down. Regrettably the helper was a coalman and his improvised towel a coalsack. The now piebald Hardy saw a rare book in a junk-shop window. When he asked the price the owner looked at him sardonically and said she didn't suppose sixpence would hurt him. 'But,' Hardy was fond of saying, 'I expect I could have got it for threepence.'

The First World War had marred Hardy's new-found serenity. He had hoped men had outlived such folly, and his visits to German and English wounded, lying a few hundred yards apart in two Dorchester hospitals, affected him deeply. Still he stoutly denied he was a pessimist, nor did those who visited him find him gloomy. Alert and courteous, interested in everything around him, a vigorous campaigner against cruelty to animals, and now, to his huge delight, a Freeman of Dorchester, he became himself a beloved part of the Wessex he had so lovingly delineated. His old age brought forth a harvest of poetry as sweet and tart as apples from an ancient tree, and his life amid the quiet countryside ended as quietly, after he had listened to his wife reading poems including Browning's *Rabbi Ben Ezra* and Walter de la Mare's *The Listeners*. He heard them all through and perhaps with his smile 'of exceptional sweetness' marked the appropriateness of de la Mare's line: 'How the silence surged softly backwards' (after the Traveller had gone), because he must have known his life was ebbing. Then his wife read from *Omar Khayaam* the verses addressed to the Creator ending:

For all the sins wherewith the face of man
Is blackened, man's forgiveness give—and take.

At this point he held up his hand for silence and not long after he died. He would probably have been intrigued by the State Funeral, replete with politicians and poets, at Westminster Abbey, but the small ceremony at Stinsford, where his heart was interred, would have pleased him more.

2

His Readers

If we are to understand any author we must learn something of the age he lived in. We shall certainly fail to read with sympathy and insight if we try to treat all literature as contemporary. Since Thomas Hardy was born when Tennyson had only just caught the public ear, when Dickens and Thackeray were at the height of their powers, and in the same year as Darwin published his *Voyage of H.M.S. Beagle*, he was obviously a Victorian through and through. When the old Queen died Hardy had already finished with the novel, and, though he was still to write hundreds of poems, his original and highly characteristic style in verse had long been firmly established and did not subsequently change.

What consequences has this for us? Clearly it's impossible to say anything useful about the Victorian age (as a whole) in a few hundred words, though it may be as well to point out that it didn't seem to have a clearly recognisable 'flavour' of its own to the Victorians, any more than our age has for us. But we ought at least to look at the effect some of the demands, beliefs and prejudices of his readers had on Hardy's work. Even today a writer who doesn't give a button for what his readers think is apt to attract precious few of them. Certainly Hardy, who had his living to earn by his pen, couldn't afford (especially at the outset of his career) to ignore his audience, even if he had wished to do so. In fact nearly all his novels show *some* signs of being tailored to the taste of the times, particularly the early ones, and we must therefore try to see what that taste was, and how it may affect our reading of Hardy.

To begin with, we have to remember that the 'reading public' of the 1860s was not at all the same thing as it is now. Education was neither free nor compulsory, so that most people couldn't read at all, while hours and conditions of work were so exhausting that many would have had no inclination to do so. In the second place, books were expensive. At one and a half guineas for a three-volume novel (the normal length) fiction was quite out of the reach of any but the fairly well-to-do, who could afford the equivalent of perhaps £10 at present-day values. There were no paper-backs and no free libraries, while the popular circulating libraries were by no means cheap. So, although conditions slowly changed during his lifetime, Hardy had to write for a middle-class public almost exclusively.

The English middle class of the day had many admirable qualities. Certainly they knew what they liked and were prepared to pay for it. Most of them spent more time on reading than we do. But what they liked was almost always a mixture of sentimentality, moral 'uplift' and continuous suspense, with a strong preference for 'happy endings', and this, as Matthew Arnold, the greatest Victorian critic, despairingly pointed out, excluded them from much of 'the best that has been thought and known in the world'. They said to the novelist—in effect— 'Entertain us or perish in the attempt', and though of course all great novelists are entertainers it isn't their only function. They also make us think, they fill us with pity or dismay, they shake our complacency, challenge our prejudices and, in short, teach us more about ourselves.

One way of lessening the cost of reading matter was to buy the quarterly or monthly magazines, in which most novels were serialised—Hardy's included. This meant providing a minor climax at the end of each instalment, and resulted in plots strung on a tangled thread of coincidence. Because magazines were for family reading the moral tone had to be impeccable; in other words vice had to be punished and virtue (if it hadn't met a noble death) rewarded. The more wealthy Victorians were also afraid of poverty, or rather the effect of it on the poor, since they thought, with considerable justification, that it might lead to revolution. Their efforts to improve matters were disorganised and piecemeal, although many of the well-to-do were acutely conscious of the shaky basis on which their prosperity rested. They could thus stomach stories like Dickens's *Christmas Carol*—which actually caused one American factory-owner to close his works on Christmas Day—but they were not prepared to listen to the great cries of pain and outrage which would have been needed to express the actual anguish and despair of millions of the working classes. They wanted stories about people like themselves, about people living in a solid, comfortable world, a world where no prostitutes swarmed outside the Haymarket in London, where children did not grow deformed at the looms in Lancashire, where match-girls did not have their jaws eaten away by sulphur, and miners never died by the hundred in underground explosions.

Some novelists gallantly defied this convention—Dickens and Mrs. Gaskell among them—but on the whole it increased in power as the owners of the lending libraries, like Mr. Mudie, constituted themselves censors of what it was proper to put in a book. What business was it of novelists to trouble their readers, who were respectable citizens, with stories of the disreputable, ragged, immoral, irreligious multitude? Didn't they sing in church (with relish, one suspects):

> The rich man in his castle,
> The poor man at his gate,
> God made them high and lowly,
> And ordered their estate.

It wasn't the function of novelists to interfere with what had been ordained from the beginning, or so they seem to have reasoned.

All this humbug was, of course, terribly frustrating to anyone who wanted to set his scenes among ordinary people, and Hardy, whose strength always lay in his depiction of the Wessex peasantry, suffered a great deal from critics who thought his country scenes were dull, vulgar and even laughable. It says much for his genius that by the end of the 19th century he had silenced this kind of criticism and was universally recognised as the great master of what Gerard Manley Hopkins called the 'Sweet especial rural scene'.

The Victorian age was one in which many people struggled up from 'Raight dahn int' cellar 'ole weer t'muck slaats on t'winders', as one sardonic comic song puts it. They were anxious, in their new-found affluence, to forget their past, and to become 'respectable'. Indeed 'respectability' became an obsession with many people, an almost magical word with many implications. One of these was the idea that sex was *not* respectable. Even to acknowledge its existence was largely forbidden, while for an author to suggest that it was of overmastering importance was perhaps the gravest fault he could commit. Marks of prudery were to be seen everywhere in contemporary fiction. Suicide was, for example, the almost inevitable destiny of unchaste women, and although Dickens spares poor Emily (in *David Copperfield*) this fate, she has to be shipped off to Australia, to remain for ever unmarried, as a result of her 'fall'. A double standard of morality existed which enabled Dickens to say (in male company) that if he 'thought his son to be particularly chaste he should be as alarmed on his account as if he could not be in good health', while preventing his biographer, Forster, from so much as hinting that Ellen Ternan (whom Dickens named first in his will) was in fact his mistress.

Still we should remember that these attempts to keep up appearances, however nauseating they seem to us, were often the product of a genuine desire to improve public behaviour, which certainly left room for it; and the hysterical outcries of disgust which often greeted novels that were to the slightest extent outspoken, were not mere hypocrisy. All the great Victorian novelists suffered to some extent from the attentions of Mrs. Grundy; Hardy, all of whose novels have to do with the loves of men and women, perhaps suffered from Grundyism more than anyone else.

A glance at Hardy's early novels reveals him attempting to come to terms with the narrow requirements of the reading public. His first book, *The Poor Man and the Lady*, was rejected because of what was called its 'wholesale blackening' of the 'aristocracy'. There was nothing frivolous about this; it was 'done in grim earnest', Hardy tells us. No wonder it was not liked. Hardy's second novel, *Desperate Remedies*, was published anonymously. It is a melodrama, obviously designed to appeal to those who wanted really sensational reading. Considering the number of wild coincidences it contains, not to mention the murder and the suicide which are necessary to bring about a 'happy ending', one might have thought that it would have sold by the thousand. In fact the reviewers hammered it, and it did not do at all well. Hardy himself never liked it much, though it does have a touch of rural humour which was to play a part in Hardy's next, and first really characteristic book, the enchanting *Under the Greenwood Tree*. This again did not sell many copies, possibly because it was firmly rooted in reality and its characters are all country-folk. 'It lacks the touch of sentiment lady novel-readers most admire,' said Hardy's publisher.

Hardy had now established himself as a novelist, and was asked to write a serial. This as he said 'proved a burden', and he disliked this form of publication with its censoring and alterations to suit the public. *A Pair of Blue Eyes*, which takes fire time and again from Hardy's own visits to Cornwall, might well have been a much better book had it not been necessary to pump excitement and coincidence into it at the expense of credibility. It suffers, too, from more than one instance of the absurdities which the fear of Mrs. Grundy could create. The worst is perhaps the scene where Elfride the heroine is asked by Knight if she had gone away with another man. She replies that she has. It would have been impossible for Hardy to have made Knight ask her directly if she had slept with the man, so he says, ' "Did you return on the same day on which you left?" "No." The word fell like a bolt from the blue and the very land and sky seemed to suffer.' Knight and Elfride are both gagged by convention from pursuing the matter so that the relatively innocent explanation doesn't emerge, and tragedy hinges on this. But the whole situation and conversation are incredible, and the description of the effect on Knight is absurdly over-pitched. Here then, the attempt both to pacify the prude and satisfy the sensationalist spoils the book, and gravely impairs Hardy's natural talent.

In his next book and one of his greatest—*Far from the Madding Crowd*—Hardy almost totally casts off all these frustrating conventions. It is the first book in which the word 'Wessex' appears, and in it he writes out of his heart of what he knew and loved. Its huge success gave him a position of strength to negotiate from, and subsequently he went his own way to a larger extent. Yet he would have done this before, given encouragement, and even so the tremendous hullaballoo about *Tess of the D'Urbervilles* and *Jude the Obscure* was still to come.

Hardy's audience, then, had a drastic effect on the shaping of his first novels, though it is true to say that the more he tried to please these readers, to avoid giving offence to the snobbish and prudish among them while satisfying those who merely wanted a 'rattling good yarn', the less he achieved success, even commercial success. Nor, at the end of the 19th century, when he was recognised as perhaps the greatest European novelist, were people any readier to accept his picture of Tess as a 'pure woman'. To Hardy purity was not something merely physical, but a state of mind. Not so to the critics. In the serial version of the novel the seduction scene was indeed cut out, and Hardy actually had to make Angel Clare use a wheelbarrow to get the milkmaids across a muddy lane—to carry them would have been improper. As for *Jude the Obscure*, the Bishop of Wakefield was so appalled by it that he threw it on the fire. Let us hope it put the fire out.

Little need be said about Hardy's poetry, nearly all of which was published after the novels, though he had written a good deal of it earlier. Poetry doesn't pay the rent and never has done. Whereas in his novels Hardy, often reluctantly and rebelliously, had to bow to the demands of his public to some extent, in his poems he never gave an inch.

3

The Poetry

Hardy always thought of himself as a poet; indeed he was often known to make disparaging remarks about 'the mechanical trade' of novel writing. He wrote poems, on and off, for nearly seventy years, to the number of almost a thousand. Some of these will certainly last as long as our language endures; his love poetry, in particular, is the most deeply moving, the most sadly perceptive of this century. All the same, his novels are what most people think of first, and those of his poems which do find a place in the anthologies are seldom his best or his most typical. If we ask why this is so we shall see that there are reasons, both good and bad, for this relative neglect, and in examining the reasons we may find our way to a better understanding of what Hardy was trying to do. For Hardy's is a singular genius; his work has a stern, stubborn integrity that is sometimes forbidding, and generally requires—like all great poetry—an effort of imaginative sympathy. Seldom does he produce anything as immediately winning as *Weathers*, with its lilting movement:

> This is the weather the cuckoo likes,
>   And so do I;

—close observation of the countryside in Spring:

> When showers betumble the chestnut spikes,
>   And nestlings fly:

and the same simple pleasure in ordinary things that those who 'sit outside at The Travellers' Rest' enjoy when

> . . . Maids come forth sprig-muslin drest,
> And citizens dream of the south and west,
>   And so do I.

Here Hardy resembles the Shakespeare of *Love's Labour's Lost*, where, in one of the concluding lyrics,

> Shepherds pipe on oaten straws,
> And merry larks are ploughman's clocks,

but neither song can be called characteristic of its author, however much we may wish both had written more in this strain.

But Hardy's characteristic strengths and his characteristic weaknesses arise in fact from a calculated refusal to write one kind of poetry—the kind exemplified in the first verse of *Weathers* just quoted—to the exclusion of another. For *Weathers* has a second verse, and just as Shakespeare goes on to tell of *Winter*,

> When icicles hang by the wall . . .
> When blood is nipped and ways be foul,

so Hardy writes of the 'weather the shepherd shuns' when

> . . . drops on gate-bars hang in a row,
> And rooks in families homeward go,

—the sodden landscape and the black lumbering birds against a lowering sky contrasting sharply with the gaiety of the first verse. In a line which he himself said was the key to much of his writing, he put it like this: 'If a way to the better there be it exacts a full look at the worst', and the 'weather' of Hardy's mind, the climate of his poetry, is predominantly that where, as in the *Winter* of the poem just quoted,

> Beeches drip in browns and duns,
>   And thresh, and ply . . .

To those who think that poetry is meant to cheer us up, who take Browning at his breeziest—in a line like, 'God's in his heaven, all's right with the world'—as a model of what poetry ought to offer, Hardy may seem a crusty old curmudgeon, gloomily intent on the miry back-alleys of human existence. This view is the result of superficial reading (something Hardy often grumbled about) and a mistaken notion of the English poetic tradition.

This tradition, Hardy's belief in it, and what he stood for in poetry are all made clear in his *Journal* for 29 May 1887. He quotes from Thomson (a minor 18th-century poet) these lines:

Thrice happy he who on the sunless side
Of a romantic mountain,
Sits coolly calm; while all the world without
Unsatisfied and sick, tosses at noon.

and comments, 'Instance of a WRONG [i.e., *selfish*] philosophy in poetry'. Now although Hardy thought this wrong, the vast majority of Victorian writers and critics, not to mention a good few poets, would have thought the idea (which is basically that poetry is a kind of *escape*) absolutely right. There is plenty of evidence. Easily the most influential 19th-century anthology was F. T. Palgrave's *Golden Treasury*, which sold enormously. Palgrave was quite uncompromising in his 1861 preface. 'Poetry,' he says, 'gives pleasures more golden than gold, leading us in higher and healthier ways than those of the world.' The editor's pious hope that the book might 'prove a storehouse of delight to Labour and Poverty' (who certainly couldn't have afforded a week's wages to buy it) is merely absurd. What it did provide was a kind of magic carpet for the middle classes, transporting them in imagination and with all possible speed, far from the harsh realities of the Industrial Revolution, to share in the experiences of Tennyson's *Lotos Eaters*, who reclined on their lost island like the 'Gods':

With half-shut eyes ever to seem
Falling asleep in a half-dream.

The Lotos (a magical herb), when eaten, removed them from all sense of involvement with humanity in general ('An ill-used race of men that cleave the soil'), and the whole poem may fairly be described as an unconscious parable of the desires of Victorian readers of poetry. Emerson, an influential American critic, summed up what was required of a poet as follows. 'The poet cannot descend into the turbid present without injury to his rarest gifts . . . nothing is of any value except the transcendental.' And this of course was just what Palgrave had tried to provide, in accordance with the advice of Tennyson's *Nightingale* who tells us that the poet should sing not of the here and now, but only

> ... of what the world will be
> When the years have passed away.

A somewhat misty prospect this, and nothing could have been further removed from Hardy's theory and practice. Railway-station waiting-rooms, insects flying into his lamp, the skeleton of an old umbrella, a second-hand suit, lines from a Borough Minute-Book, a pair of boots even, and in his old age a passing motor-car—all are for him equally the stuff of poetry. Nothing is 'poetic', unless life itself is poetic.

Hardy was in good company, and had grounds for including, in Coleridge's phrase:

> All thoughts, all passions, all delights
> Whatever stirs this mortal frame,

in his work. It was the adolescent Keats, fluent producer of poetic candy-floss, whom the Victorians most admired. But when, older and made wise through suffering, Keats asks in *The Fall of Hyperion* how the 'throne' of the highest poetry may be reached, he is told:

> 'None can usurp this height,' returned that shade,
> 'But those to whom the miseries of the world
> Are misery and will not let them rest'.

147–9

If we object to Hardy's choice of subject we shall have to object to Chaucer's, to Shakespeare's, to Wordsworth's, and indeed to Tennyson's (who was much too great a poet to stick to his own theories) on the same grounds.

Bound up with the question of subject, of course, is the question of style, and any distinction between them is likely to be artificial. It will be best, however, to admit at once that this is where Hardy has come in for most attack and also where it is most difficult to defend him. For Hardy has the unenviable distinction of having written some of the worst lines and a few of the most inept poems that any great English poet has ever

32

produced. It is, regrettably, quite easy to quote. There is, for instance, the collapse repeatedly brought about by changing from a dignified to an all-too-everyday vocabulary (in a rather weak poem here, admittedly):

> We late-lamented, resting here,
> Are mixed to human jam.

Then there is the choice of a metre altogether wrong for the mood of the poem. Here a lyric of sad reflection has the jingling, cantering lines:

> I would be candid willingly, but dawn draws on so chillingly
> As to render further cheerlessness intolerable now.

This might have been written by Gilbert for Sullivan to set to music. Sometimes, too, it has to be admitted that Hardy simply cuts prose up into lengths. For example, who would care to mark the breaks in: 'Man, you too, aren't you one of these rough followers of the criminal; all hanging about to hear how he is going to bear examination in the hall.' Yet these are the first two and a half lines of a poem on St. Peter (*In the Servants' Quarters*). Then there are the lines that can only be called asthmatic, the result of a struggle to squeeze too much in, of which the last line of a poem (on the wax-work of a fiddler at Madame Tussaud's!) is typical:

> Yes, gamuts that graced forty years' flight were not a small thing

In this line too is an example of Hardy's sometimes eccentric and always highly individual vocabulary. He believed (like Alice's Humpty Dumpty) that words should be shown who was 'master'. 'Gamuts' (here used in a technical, musical sense) would fox most readers, and Hardy produces a fair number of similar jaw-crackers. He is also too fond of 'dictionary' words like 'ditty', 'terrene', 'beldame' and 'thuswise', for instance, and he can say, most unfortunately, 'Where the sun *ups it*, mist-imbued', when what he *means* is 'rises'. It was always easy to criticise this mannerism (which is, however, not nearly as widespread as some critics suggest). But Hardy's failures are merely the price we have to pay for what G. M. Young called

'[Hardy's] ancient music . . . this gnarled and wintry phrasing'. In return for enduring them we receive wonderful glowing phrases like 'the foam-fingered sea', the 'Isle by the Race, many-caverned, bald, wrinkled of face', and single adjectives as telling as 'mothy' in the phrase 'mothy curfew-tide'. Here, 'curfew-tide' is also Hardy's invention and rings absolutely true. Instances could be multiplied, and Hardy can produce things as sonorously dignified as this from a sonnet, *The Schreckhorn, with thoughts of Leslie Stephen*:

> And the eternal essence of his mind
> Enter this silent adamantine shape,

or phrases like 'Oblivion's swallowing sea' (which Shakespeare somehow omitted from his plays). There are also lyrics picked bare of all but the simplest words, like this (the title is the first line given):

> I found her out there
> On a slope few see,
> That falls westwardly
> To the salt-edged air,
> Where the ocean breaks
> On the purple strand,
> And the hurricane shakes
> The solid land.

It is worth noticing how much of the force of 'hurricane' is gained from the framework of plain English around it. Incidentally, the whole poem is one of Hardy's best. In this matter of vocabulary then, Hardy is so often whang in the gold that we can accept a number of ill-aimed shafts as inevitable.

We cannot quite leave it there, however, because Hardy vigorously defended his own idiosyncrasies. It was no accident that he wrote as he did, but the result of set purpose on his part. He took his stand firmly (perhaps too firmly) on one side of an age-old controversy about style and content in poetry, and it is to this that we must now turn briefly.

When Pope defined true wit in poetry as 'What oft was thought but ne'er so well expressed', he was simply placing all the emphasis on the *way* in which the poet conveys what he has to say. (The substance, it is implied, doesn't matter much.) When Wordsworth spoke of the poet's duty to 'keep [his] eye on the object' before anything else, and Matthew Arnold (whose cast of mind was very like Hardy's indeed) says poets should 'strive . . . to see the thing as in itself it really is', they are taking up the opposite position, arguing that it is *what* is said that matters most. It is clear which side Hardy took, since he quotes these remarks of Wordsworth and Arnold with enthusiasm, and gives his own opinion that the secret of poetry lies in 'seeing into the *heart* of a thing, which [is] realism in fact'. If we bear in mind also what he said—in a letter to Edmund Gosse in 1918—to the effect that his instinct had always been 'to avoid the jewelled line in poetry, as being effeminate', we shall be well on the way to understanding Hardy's attitude.

As to why he should have taken it up in the first place, one can venture a guess. Tennyson was perhaps the greatest exponent of the 'jewelled' line in English; certainly the possessor of a faultless ear and an endless supply of melodious phrases. Such tuneful feats as—

The moan of doves in immemorial elms
And murmuring of innumerable bees

—were on everyone's lips in the later 19th century. Tennyson dominated the poetic landscape, he was a poet both great and various, and it was impossible to ignore him. Hardy didn't ignore him; in fact he greatly admired him; but from the very beginning he was determined to 'go and do otherwise'. Indeed he could be decidedly cross-grained in his rejection of anything 'jewelled'. Tennyson would very likely have admired *In Front of the Landscape*, with its striking picture of

. . . a headland of hoary aspect
    Gnawed by the tide,
Frilled by the nimb of the morning,

where the unusual vocabulary (nimb = mist) is part of the ghostly effect. But what would he have made of the 'faces' in the same poem:

. . . Some as with slow-born tears that brinily trundled

35

[down them]? This is striking; it is, if you think about it, apt, yet it is anything but 'jewelled', taking away all the glamour of tears as crystals or dew-drops or pearls. And elsewhere at times Hardy uses his 'facts' like cudgels to knock the stuffing out of a poem. For instance, to begin a lyric in the manner of the Elizabethans:

'Why do you weep there, O sweet lady
Why do you weep before that brass?'

and then to inform us superfluously, disastrously and parenthetically that 'I'm a mere student sketching the mediaeval' is pretty unforgivable. Yet far more often than not, Hardy is right in his aim, and far more often than not he achieves it. There is no line more glittering than Hardy's recollection of Beeny Cliff and his lost love after forty-three years: 'O the opal and the sapphire of that wandering western sea'; and the use of jewels for the gleaming colours, opal for the ever-changing sun-lit water, sapphire for the dark blue shadow, the long roll of the line, the heavy alliteration (O-opal, sapphire-sea, wandering-western) and the striking epithet 'wandering'—Hardy is always first-class on the sea—all add to the warmth and brilliance of the picture. But the next line is a test case. It runs:

And the woman riding high above with bright hair flapping free.

Now the word 'flapping' is decidedly not the one that most of us would choose. It has associations with clothes on the line and with the more ungainly birds. We should probably pick 'flowing' or 'floating', and Hardy must have been very tempted by the second because his wife in her *Recollections* had left him a sketch of this very scene when she talks of 'my hair floating in the wind'. But he must have remembered better than even she did, with an astonishing clarity and precision. Phrases from another poem, *Lying Awake*,

You, Morningtide Star, now are steady-eyed, over the east,
    I know it as if I saw you;
You, Beeches, engrave on the sky your thin twigs, even the least,
    Had I paper and pencil I'd draw you . . .

illustrate perfectly this essential quality of Hardy's poetry. It is more than nostalgia, viewing the past through rose-coloured spectacles; it is an ability to recreate, to re-explore the past, as if it were still the present. Time in all Hardy's poetry (as in Shakespeare's sonnets) is the Enemy. But if Memory is distorted for whatever reason, either to comfort or ennoble, or simply for the sake of 'melody', the cause of truth and poetry is betrayed, and Time has triumphed. Hardy describes his wife standing on Dundagel Head, in another poem,

> As a wind-tugged tress
> Flapped her cheek like a flail.

When he wrote this he might have said, as he does elsewhere, 'I see it as if I were there'. What he saw was what actually happens. On a high cliff the wind is never steady, but irregular, blowing in swirls and gusts, so that long, heavy ringleted hair doesn't 'flow' or 'float' but does in fact 'flap'. It may seem niggling to insist upon so small a matter, but this is the indispensable clue to an understanding of Hardy. The antagonism of Time and Memory and the endless stress upon truth to the actual experience are the essential ingredients of his poetic art. If we want poetry tailored according to what 'sounds' or 'looks' best, or what readers are used to, we must go elsewhere. 'Real poets,' wrote John Clare in the year of Hardy's birth, 'must be truly honest men.' His own supremely truthful pictures of the countryside were ruthlessly altered by his prudish publisher, and because he portrayed such scenes as that of a field-mouse disturbed by reapers, bolting out 'With all her young ones hanging on her teats', he was thought a coarse peasant, and left unread (though not by Hardy). Wilfred Owen's terrible pictures of war arose out of his conviction that 'true poets must be truthful'. 'The poetry,' he added, 'is in the pity.' It is with men like these that Hardy belongs; those who refuse to pick over their experience and select from it on any ground whatever, especially that of what is or isn't pleasing to the ear of the conventional reader. Against this tendency Hardy set himself to struggle, and that his struggles are sometimes ungainly, his vocabulary ill-chosen and his subject-matter dreary, cannot be denied. But we don't expect perfect balance from a rebellious intellect, and even at his worst Hardy was a useful corrective.

Perhaps it would be fair now to look at Hardy treating one of those edifying moral anecdotes which crop up so often in Victorian poetry. (Tennyson's *Enoch Arden* is the classic example but there are many others.) In *The Curate's Kindness: A Workhouse Irony*, an old man tells the story as the waggon carrying him jogs on to the Institution where 'peace is assured' because:

> The men in one wing and their wives in another
> Is strictly the rule of the Board.

Just as they arrive the well-meaning young curate rushes up to announce that he has persuaded the Guardians to abolish this rule. As he joyfully cries:

> Old folks, that harsh order is altered,
> Be not sick of heart.

the old man's heart sinks. He has not, after all, escaped his 'forty years chain', and (an added irony) it is too late now even for him, as he puts it, to

> . . . go back and drown me
> At Pummery or Ten-Hatches Weir.

There are two points to notice here. First is the depth of Hardy's insight. Life is, he suggests, essentially ironic. Here cruelty to one arises from genuine kindness to many—the rule *was* inhumane—the other old couples *will* mostly be happy, though, as he intended, our sympathies go to the old man. Secondly, the *situation* would have been meat and drink to any number of poets. One can easily imagine some follower of Tennyson at work on the conclusion to *A Poor Law Romance*:

> . . . Then the good old pair,
> United by the curate's urgent plea
> Blessed him and one another. So they dwelt
> For many a year in mellow happiness,
> To cease at last upon the self-same day.

Poetry like this fails to realise the tragic alternatives implicit in every human situation. Hardy saw more clearly. Life to him was a walk on a razor-edge, love and happiness were accordingly infinitely precarious yet infinitely worthwhile, and in all his greatest poems this quality of fragility is present, as we shall see when we come to consider the love poems of 1913 and later. In the meantime enough has, I hope, been said to show the variety of Hardy's work, something of his poetic theory and practice, what marks his individuality as a poet, and, most important, to demonstrate his unfailing devotion to ideals which must often have seemed his alone. But it is, in any case, high time to leave generalising and look more particularly at what Hardy actually wrote.

CLASSIFYING HARDY'S POEMS

Here at the outset we run into a minor difficulty. I have said that Hardy wrote poetry for nearly seventy years. But he only published it for about thirty years, and when he began to do so (in 1898, with *Wessex Poems*, of which there were only fifty-one), he had a very large backlog to make up. He hadn't bothered to date many of his earlier poems (nor did he ever take much trouble over this), and anyway he constantly revised and generally improved his work, both poetry and prose, over the years; sometimes taking up and finishing a poem from a rough draft of many years before. Consequently we cannot hope to look at Hardy's poems in chronological order—a method which is often convenient—and, to make matters more difficult still, we know that Hardy destroyed a good many early poems which dissatisfied him. Any attempt, then, to trace his development in an orderly fashion is likely to fail.

The alternative is to try to group the poems in some way, so that like can be discussed with like. The obvious way to set about this is to classify them according to subject and theme. This is a tricky business, of course, and the categories I shall suggest are only tentative. The order which follows here is largely one of convenience, with the more important work coming later. It can be taken for granted that there is a large degree of overlap between categories.

1. *Formal poetry:* Here Hardy is working inside the poetic conventions of his time, producing sonnets, epigrams and translations which are more or less 'traditional' in form and treatment, if not in content.

2. *Narrative poetry:* The principal (not always the only) aim here is to tell a story. For subjects Hardy uses both topical anecdotes and legends of the past, writing mainly in ballad form or in blank verse.

3. *Satirical poetry:* These are what Hardy called 'Human Shows'. They are direct and often acid attacks upon human folly and humbug, in which Hardy sets out to criticise something he dislikes intensely.

4. *Philosophical poetry:* The term 'philosophical' is used fairly strictly here to denote poems which take the form of 'obstinate questionings', as Hardy called them, of Fate, the existence and nature of God, human suffering and similar puzzles. Here Hardy's primary purpose is to explore these matters and often to propound solutions as well.

5. *Reflective poetry:* By far the largest category, these are what Hardy generally called 'Reveries'. I have subdivided them within this category according to their subjects. In these poems Hardy is content to ponder, to meditate, on some person, memory or chance occurrence, not attempting to establish a chain of reasoning or to find an 'answer', concerned rather to allow the thing considered to make its own point than to 'work it out' for the reader.

6. *Love poetry:* Again a very large group, and again subdivided, this category hardly needs further comment at this point.

FORMAL POETRY

There are a number of odds and ends of translation of which little need be said except that, just as in Walter de la Mare's poem 'Whatever Miss T. eats turns into Miss T.', so whatever Hardy translates turns into Thomas Hardy. Some lines from Sophocles however provided Hardy with the framework of a fine sonnet—not published until 1956—which dwells with unrelieved darkness of mood upon old age, like a headland

> Where sunshine, bird and bloom frequent no more
> And cowls of cloud wrap the stars' radiancy.

It is a fine, sombre conclusion, and reminds us that Hardy's sonnets, of which he wrote more than forty, have generally been undervalued. Some of his attempts at this supremely difficult form are among the few really good sonnets the late 19th century produced, and it is interesting to see how, even when he was trying his hardest to write like Shakespeare, and getting within reasonable distance of doing so in lines like:

> Numb as a vane that cankers on its point,
> True to the wind that kissed ere canker came,

he cannot keep out ideas and expressions as uniquely his own as:

> . . . Sportsman Time but rears his brood to kill,

(where the lovers are most unromantically compared with partridges, and Time, perhaps more effectively, becomes the gamekeeper).

The Minute before Meeting is easily Hardy's finest love sonnet. Later in date than the others, its fine 'onset' (sonnets, like sprinters, need to get off to a good start) and strong, marching alliteration are apparent in the first lines:

> The grey gaunt days dividing us in twain
> Seemed hopeless hills my strength must faint to climb.

They remind us slightly of Shakespeare, it is true, but they have their own easy strength. The second quatrain is subtle and 'witty' with its assured word-play, and its long closing line— 'On my long need while these slow blank months passed'— suggesting in its plodding monosyllables the dragging weight of time spent in hope. The conclusion, with its anguished conviction that the long-awaited meeting will be spoiled by its brevity, will not yield a 'full-up measure of felicity', is moving, but a bit neurotic. It is only later, when Hardy turns the sonnet to his own characteristic purposes, that he achieves complete success.

In *A Church Romance, Mellstock, circa 1835*, he recreates his mother's first encounter with his father. It is written with a flowing ease that makes one wish Hardy hadn't abandoned this form, as he did in later life. His picture of the silhouetted 'music-men' in the gloomy gallery neatly stresses the importance of the music and its 'message', just as the phrase 'strenuous viol's inspirer' points the intensity of the playing. By contrast with the swiftly sketched story of the first eight lines, the last six are quiet and reflective:

> Thus their heart's bond began, in due time signed.
> And long years thence, when Age had scared Romance,
> At some old attitude of his or glance
> That gallery-scene would break upon her mind,
> With him as minstrel, ardent, young, and trim,
> Bowing 'New Sabbath' or 'Mount Ephraim'.

Here is a wry honesty and quiet charm, deriving in part from the homely phrasing, in part from the absence of sentimentality. We may read a good deal of Hardy in this too; his own memory was continually open to receive, in 'some old attitude . . . or glance' the hint that could lead to a 'moment of vision'. Many of his poems 'break upon the mind' in just this way, like a random shaft of light falling on some forgotten ruin, lighting it up for a moment so that we can see it as it was in its heyday. It is worth remarking here that it is only Romance that Age has scared. Love might last, but not its first illusion of perfection, and Hardy manages to suggest here, without actually stating it, that between his mother and father there was an enduring, yet not blind love.

I have already mentioned Hardy's sonnet, *The Schreckhorn, with thoughts of Leslie Stephen*. This has a good claim to be considered the finest climbers' poem ever written. Hardy was obviously impressed by the fierce peak, but he doesn't make the mistake of trying to describe it. Instead he invests it with a 'personality' and thus subtly conveys the queer, almost mystical relationship that exists between men and the mountains they are drawn to climb. Stephen, Hardy's friend, was a fine but severe critic, besides being one of the foremost Alpinists of his time. The last six lines must be quoted in full not only for their deep feeling and severe dignity, but also for the lovely closing image, which is not at all typical of Hardy, yet is here singularly apt.

> At his last change, when Life's dull coils unwind,
> Will he, in old love, hitherward escape,
> And the eternal essence of his mind
> Enter this silent adamantine shape,
> And his low voicing haunt its slipping snows
> When dawn that calls the climber dyes them rose?

Stephen's own phrase for the Schreckhorn, which he was the first to climb, was 'the grimmest fiend of the Oberland', but Hardy could see beyond this to the 'old love' which drew his friend to the mountains, in part perhaps because they represented a kind of eternity he could believe in, for he was, like Hardy, an agnostic. This is perhaps the most completely successful of Hardy's sonnets. Others, however, deserve a mention— notably *At a Lunar Eclipse, Barthelemon at Vauxhall, A Wet Night* (which is a tribute to his ancestors), and the sombre *We are getting to the end* (almost his last poem)—not to mention a revealing one written in the First World War, where Hardy reflects on the similarities between Dorset and German speech forms and the senselessness of the fighting then in progress. It is, however, because I want to emphasise that Hardy could, when he chose, write supremely well, without eccentricities, in this most difficult form, that I have spent some time discussing his sonnets. There was nothing of the 'primitive' about him, and those critics who have from time to time sneered at his lack of 'formal education' ought to be able to show who, in the late 19th century, wrote better sonnets than Hardy, to sustain their charge. They will not find it easy.

NARRATIVES AND ANECDOTES

Hardy wrote over 160 poems in this category. Some are several pages long and they are scattered fairly evenly throughout his *Collected Poems*. Poets are not always their own best judges, and Hardy viewed his own narratives with more affection than was altogether wise. They are by far the weakest of his works, all with this in common, that whether they are mere sketches of a situation or complete stories, Hardy is merely the narrator, uninvolved personally in what is happening. Perhaps this is the reason why they are so seldom compelling. For though Hardy shared in full measure the villager's taste for gossip, when his own feelings are not aroused his writing often becomes either flat or meandering, or both.

There are exceptions, of course. They occur whenever Hardy is able to enter imaginatively into the incident, to infuse it with his own experience. Thus, when he read these lines from a Budmouth (i.e. Weymouth) Minute-Book: 'It being deposed that VII women who were mayds before he knew them have been brought upon the towne [rates] by the fornications of one Ralph Blossom, Mr. Mayor inquired why he should not contribute XIV pence weekly toward their mayntenance. But it being shown that the sayd R.B. was dying of a purple feaver, no order was made'—they revealed the past, like a mirror which flashed back at him that blaze of passion which had once lit up the lives of the long-dead actors now remembered only on this dusty page. Hardy pictures each woman in turn answering Ralph Blossom, who speaks to them out of 'Hell or some such place'. Their replies vary from amusingly coy protestation:

> 'I did not understand your sign!'
> Will be the words of Caroline;

ONE RALPH BLOSSOM SOLILOQUIZES

t o dry acceptance:

> And Rosa: 'I feel no hostility,
> For I must own I lent facility'.

But Hardy's own conviction, which he always kept, that love is, at any rate potentially, the 'crown of existence', bursts out in the last six lines:

And Anne cries: 'O the time was fair,
So wherefore should you burn down there?
There is a deed under the sun, my Love,
And that was ours. What's done is done, my Love.
These trumpets here in Heaven are dumb to me
With you away. Dear, come, O come to me!'

Here is an eloquent simplicity, rising to splendidly arrogant defiance: 'These trumpets here in Heaven are dumb to me', and falling away in tenderness: 'Dear, come, O come to me!' But this isn't really a narrative at all, of course: it's Hardy himself speaking, though with an exultant note seldom heard in his own love poetry. Only when he can identify himself in this way does he fully succeed.

1. *Hardy and the folk-song tradition*. When Hardy tells a story in the folk-song or ballad convention—something he did too seldom, perhaps distrusting his own facility—he *can* strike the authentic note. *The Dark-Eyed Gentleman*, for instance, and *The Orphaned Old Maid* have the uninhibited gusto of Burns's songs, and *Julie-Jane* is genuinely moving with its sad yet wry ending:

> Bubbling and brightsome eyed!
> But now—O never again.
> She chose her bearers before she died
> From her fancy-men.

As in all the best folk-songs, sorrow is implied, not dwelt on, and sex is spoken of frankly but without a snigger.

2. *Dialect poems*. Hardy's few dialect narratives are easily his best, probably because in them he handles conversation so much more deftly than in, for example, *At Wynyard's Gap*, where he bumbles away as follows for several pages:

> SHE
> Put up? Do you think so!
> HE
> I incline to such,
> My *dear* (do you mind?)
> SHE
> Yes—Well (*more softly*), I don't much.

Corporal Tullidge's Tale of Valenciennes and that good-humoured romp, *The Bridenight Fire*, are both much better than this. They gain a good deal from their Wessex phrasing, as does the pick of the bunch, *The Homecoming*, which is quite unlike any other poem I have read. The efforts of the rough old farmer from 'haunted Toller Down' to pacify his scared young bride are both amusing and touching:

> 'Now don't ye rub your eyes so red; we're home and have no cares;
> Here's a skimmer-cake for supper, peckled onions, and some pears;
> I've got a little keg o' summat strong, too, under stairs.'

and the haunting refrain of the wind outside is weirdly exciting.

SATIRICAL POEMS

Much of Hardy's poetry can of course be called satirical in a general way. But it is a mistake to confuse what springs from his often disenchanted attitude towards life, from a mind attuned to probing the realities that lie behind the outward 'seemings' of mankind, with satire in the strict sense. This sets out to expose human folly and humbug by ruthlessly stripping away all its pretensions, and it is with those poems where Hardy deliberately puts a fierce cutting-edge on his irony, where it is his set intention to hurt and shock the conventionally-minded, that we are now concerned. It seems to me that these are among the finest poems of their kind (a kind not greatly in favour with the Victorians, and since the 18th century much under-rated). There are not very many of them, but the best have a concentrated venom and a polished, icy wit which is unique for the period.

Perhaps the best is *The Ruined Maid*, a dialogue which neatly knocks out that keystone of Victorian sexual morality, the idea that a 'fallen woman' *must* be both unhappy and ultimately doomed to a miserable death. Fresh from the country, Melia's former friend is flabbergasted by her one-time workmate's prosperity and questions her:

> "You left us in tatters, without shoes or socks,
> Tired of digging potatoes, and spudding up docks;

And now you've gay bracelets and bright feathers three!"—
"Yes, that's how we dress when we're ruined," said she.

—"At home in the barton you said 'thee' and 'thou',
And 'thik oon', and 'theäs oon' and 't'other'; but now
Your talking quite fits 'ee for high compa-ny"—
"Some polish is gained with one's ruin," said she.

The gawking wonderment of the one and the yawning, off-hand
poise of the other are here beautifully pointed, and so—it
is easy to miss—is the misery of the starved, half-enslaved farm-
worker. The 'jolly ploughboy' and the 'merry milkmaid'
were favourite Victorian myths, but Hardy knew (none better)
that rural poverty was as desperate as any. The whole poem—
well read aloud—is both very funny and, upon consideration,
a deeply sympathetic piece of social criticism. As for the conclusion:

—"I wish I had feathers, a fine sweeping gown,
And a delicate face, and could strut about Town!"—
"My dear—a raw country girl, such as you be,
Cannot quite expect that. You ain't ruined," said she.

not only has it outstanding 'bite' and neatness of finish, but it
also reveals how much convention relies on 'labels'—for what,
Hardy asks, does 'ruined' really mean? *The Christening*, with its
picture of a baby so beautiful that:

At so superb a thing
The congregation smile
And turn their heads awhile.

suggests, even more shockingly for the time, that wedlock itself
may not be everyone's choice. The mother's reply to the
question:

"Where is the baby's father?"

is unexpected. He has not deserted her (and 'serve her right for
trusting him' would be the expected moral), he is

47

"In the woods afar.
He says there is none he'd rather
Meet under moon or star
Than me, of all that are.

"To clasp me in lovelike weather.
    Wish fixing when . . ."

This reminds us of Dylan Thomas's Polly Garter in *Under Milk
Wood* with her 'Oh isn't life a terrible thing, thank God!', and
perhaps the phrase

This gem of the race
The decent fain would smother

refers not only to the baby itself in its innocent beauty but also,
indirectly, to love itself. Maybe Hardy implies here that love
isn't really respectable in the eyes of 'respectable persons'. His
phrase for marriage—'Slovening/As vulgar man and wife'—is
not what most readers would like to hear.

In *Ah, are you digging on my grave* Hardy points a picture of
the kind much admired at the Royal Academy of his day. A
'little dog' is digging on his mistress's grave. One can readily
imagine the caption 'Faithful unto death'. But Hardy has another
point to make, an exposure, sad rather than sour, of a human
illusion. He uses the ballad convention of *The Unquiet Grave*—a
dialogue between living and dead. Finally the dead woman says:

"Ah, yes! *You* dig upon my grave . . .
    Why flashed it not on me
That one true heart was left behind! . . ."

But the little dog replies:

"Mistress, I dug upon your grave
    To bury a bone . . .
I am sorry, but I quite forgot
    It was your resting place."

There is no comfort here at all. It is utterly merciless, as are a
whole group of poems, *Satires of Circumstance*, in which Hardy
shows us the cross-currents of envy, conceit and pride beneath

the peaceful surface of such everyday events as a tea-party. After a brilliant sermon, a 'Bible-class' pupil who 'adores' the preacher as one 'without gloss or guile' sees her 'idol'

> ... re-enact at the vestry-glass
> Each pulpit gesture in deft dumb-show
> That had moved the congregation so.

In his last four collections, Hardy wrote nothing of this kind. Yet this small group of poems reveals Hardy as possessing both the precision of aim and the controlled strength of feeling needed for success in this difficult kind of work.

PHILOSOPHIC POEMS

Hardy repeatedly disclaimed any intention of setting up as a philosopher. Nevertheless he was extraordinarily well-read in both ancient and modern philosophy, giving us in *Drinking Song* a good-humoured, potted history of philosophy and philosophers from Thales to Einstein with his: '. . . notion/That there's no Time, nor Space, nor Motion.' Indeed he even begins a poem, remarkably entitled *Our Old Friend Dualism*, with the even more remarkable lines:

> All hail to him, the Protean! A tough old chap is he:
> Spinoza and the Monists cannot make him cease to be.

It's true that poetry can be made out of anything, but this is surely rather a rarefied atmosphere for most readers, and similar scraps of imperfectly digested philosophy litter a good many of Hardy's pages. I don't mean that Hardy didn't understand the philosophers himself, of course; merely that he seldom succeeds in incorporating these matters fluently in his verse. According to Walter Bagehot, Milton's chief mistake was that he 'made God argue'. Hardy (who himself prefaces a poem with this remark) regrettably went one better than Milton and on numerous occasions made God chat, like some 'remote and ineffectual don' in doggerel phrases like this:

> I mean, of course, well knowing
> Thy present conformation

But a unit of my tentatives,
Whereof such heaps lie blowing . . .

A PHILOSOPHICAL FANTASY

Whether Hardy meant it seriously or as a 'send-up' doesn't much matter. It is tedious stuff.

Hardy had in fact embarked very early on a quest to resolve a conflict in himself. His emotional attachment was to 'that bright believing band' of Christians, to whose cry of:

        . . . "Hark! hark!
    The glorious distant sea! . . ."

(an indirect reference to the 'evidence' for God's existence), he can only reply:

            . . . Alas, 'tis but yon dark
    And wind-swept pine to me!

Opposed to this was his intellectual conviction that some

        . . . Vast Imbecility,
    Mighty to build and blend,
    But impotent to tend,
    Framed us in jest, and left us now to hazardry?

NATURE'S QUESTIONING

In him, to borrow A. E. Housman's lines, intellect and emotion

    . . . cease not fighting, east and west
    On the marches of my breast.

None of those poems, however, in which this conflict is hauled into the foreground, is particularly memorable. Though they contain striking phrases they are seldom wholly satisfactory, and probably this is because Hardy is usually gravelled by the impossibility of getting what he wants to say into a non-technical vocabulary. When he remarks (not very elegantly), 'That which I fain would wot of shuns my sense', we are tempted to murmur disrespectfully, 'Ours too'.

REFLECTIVE POEMS

However, Hardy wrote many poems in which he doesn't attempt to sort out the problems of existence, but merely poses a question, or muses on his own place among 'souls in bond'. Generally quiet and meditative in tone, though sometimes anguished, these poems are rarely far from an acceptance, sad and reluctant though it may be, of the world as it is, and these I should like to call 'Reflective poems' because in them Hardy is musing rather than arguing. They include some of his greatest work.

In *A Night of Questioning* Hardy begins as splendidly as he ever did:

> On the eve of All-Souls' Day
> I heard the dead men say
> Who lie by the tottering tower,
> To the dark and doubling wind
> At the midnight's turning hour,
> When other speech had thinned:
> 'What of the world now?'

and pursues the question, repeated by those 'swayed in the sunk sea-bed' and 'the troubled skulls that heave/And fust in the flats of France', to whom the wind always returns the same answer, that the world is the same as ever. The complex rhythm of the poem, turning and twisting like the doubling wind itself, and simple, often biblical, language give this poem power and dignity. Its characteristic mark is that kind of heroic hopelessness which also occurs in Hardy's three fine poems where he states his own stoic position:

> Black is night's cope;
> But death will not appal
> One who, past doubtings all,
> Waits in unhope.

The three poems are collectively entitled *In Tenebris* (In Obscurity, or perhaps just In Darkness), and all have a dark power, dramatic force, and unforgettable phrasing.

Hardy's attitude in his Reflective Poems. It is one of the hallmarks of Hardy's 'reveries', as he called them, that they don't all arrive inevitably at the same gloomy conclusion. He looked back wistfully at his own childhood, and children often arouse in him a serenity and even a hopefulness of mood. Thus he sees himself at *The Afternoon Service at Mellstock* 'mindlessly singing' a Tate-and-Brady psalm, but, as he says,

> . . . I am not aware
> That I have gained by subtle thought on things
> Since we stood psalming there.

This is, if you like, simply nostalgic, but there is elsewhere a feeling of intense wonder, even awe, which colours a number of other poems. Taken together they suggest that Hardy retained something of that child's-eye vision which Wordsworth possessed. Hardy doesn't make this an article of faith: it isn't his prevailing mood by any means. Nevertheless such glimpses as those in *The Year's Awakening*, where striking astronomical images are contrasted with the mystery of a crocus's 'fore-knowledge' of spring, the vision (in *The Blinded Bird*) of the lark singing without hatred in 'Eternal dark. . . . Who hath Charity? This bird', and the famous glimpse of *The Oxen* which, legend says, 'kneel' on 'Christmas Eve, and twelve of the clock', with its infinitely humble conclusion, 'I should go with him in the gloom/Hoping it might be so', all reveal a man who doesn't profess to understand creation or to condemn it out of hand, but is swayed at times by old belief or sudden perception into a puzzled acceptance or half-understanding. Surely Hardy put part of himself into the 'journeying boy' (in *Midnight on the Great Western*) with its beautiful conclusion:

> Knows your soul a sphere, O journeying boy,
> Our rude realms far above,
> Whence with spacious vision you mark and mete
> This region of sin that you find you in,
> But are not of?

suggesting, perhaps, in the almost Christ-like innocence of the boy travelling towards a world unknown, that here is a glimpse of man as he might be.

It would be easy to press this side of Hardy's work too far. Still, one of Hardy's greatest poems, *The Darkling Thrush*, may be discussed here since, among other things, it so overwhelmingly refutes Chesterton's clever and facile gibe at Hardy as 'the village atheist brooding and blaspheming over the village idiot'. I quote the whole of the poem because no one would deny that it is a masterpiece and because it so well demonstrates Hardy's mastery of the 'mechanics' of poetry; the art and science of putting a poem together, which is a skill often denied him.

> I leant upon a coppice gate
>   When Frost was spectre-gray,
> And Winter's dregs made desolate
>   The weakening eye of day.
> The tangled bine-stems scored the sky
>   Like strings of broken lyres,
> And all mankind that haunted nigh
>   Had sought their household fires.
>
> The land's sharp features seemed to be
>   The Century's corpse outleant,
> His crypt the cloudy canopy,
>   The wind his death-lament.
> The ancient pulse of germ and birth
>   Was shrunken hard and dry,
> And every spirit upon earth
>   Seemed fervourless as I.
>
> At once a voice arose among
>   The bleak twigs overhead
> In a full-hearted evensong
>   Of joy illimited;
> An aged thrush, frail, gaunt and small,
>   In blast-beruffled plume,
> Had chosen thus to fling his soul
>   Upon the growing gloom.
>
> So little cause for carolings
>   Of such ecstatic sound
> Was written on terrestrial things
>   Afar or nigh around,
> That I could think there trembled through
>   His happy good-night air
> Some blessed Hope, whereof he knew
>   And I was unaware.

Here, first of all, is the typical Hardy landscape opening, notable for its precision, with its 'spectre-gray frost' and also its awareness, shown in 'winter's dregs' and 'tangled bine-stems', that the rubbish of last summer lends an added desolation to the scene. 'All mankind', too, is excluded. At the same time Hardy conveys the dispiriting quality of what he sees in 'the weakening eye of day' (for the sun), and by distorting a favourite Romantic image, the lyre, suggesting lyric poetry. He hints too at some eerie quality, by using words like 'spectre-gray' and 'haunted nigh'. Thus he makes a number of points simultaneously, creating a terrible over-all bleakness and emptiness of impression.

The apparently dead landscape is now turned neatly into a symbol of the dead century. A series of comparisons is used, each quite unforced, yet each more withering than the last (until life itself, 'the ancient pulse of germ and birth', is frozen—a frightening concept) and Hardy falls away into a flat statement, utterly dispirited and dispiriting, of his own inner despair. The remarkable thing about the third verse is the way in which Hardy refuses all temptation to overstate the contrast it contains with what has gone before. True, Hardy gives a wonderful vibrant warmth to the thrush's song by his use of words like 'full-hearted', even suggesting in the adjective 'illimited' that the song is some kind of universal symbol of hope. But—and this seems to me a touchstone of Hardy's genius—the thrush itself (the point is hammered home) is 'aged', 'frail', 'gaunt' and 'small'. It is in fact very much like the poet himself perhaps, 'blast-beruffled', yet in this cruel weather (for frost is death to birds) it can fling its soul into its song. There is no attempt here to pull out any of the obvious Romantic stops (this isn't a 'wise thrush' like Browning's, singing in a 'first, fine careless rapture', nor does Hardy make it more than a bird, like Shelley's 'Skylark': 'Hail to thee, blithe spirit,/Bird thou never wert'). It is clearly only in a figurative sense that it 'flings its soul' into its song. So, because we can totally accept the truth of the incident related, we can also accept Hardy's musings on the significance of what he saw and heard. Though he stresses again in 'carolings' and 'ecstatic' the beauty of the song, he at once refers us back to the deathly scene, and only then offers a tentative 'conclusion'. Again there is the refusal to overstate: 'I *could* think . . . there *trembled* through,' he says. It is the way Hardy is driven, against all the evidence of his senses, to accept the possibility, however faint, of 'some blessed hope', the perfect balance between reason and emotion in the poem, the contrast between the deathless beauty of the music and the deathstruck setting for it, with, perhaps above all else, the hesitance, the shyness almost, with which Hardy advances his infinitely precarious conclusion, that make this a great poem. Whether we accept the 'hope' as justified or not, the image of the thrush remains, gallant and unconquerable, an image of man himself 'slighted but enduring'.

The problem of Hardy's wide range of subjects. At this point distinctions between 'kinds' of poems begin to blur. Hardy's sharp, curious wide-ranging eye falls upon many little-noticed things, and he can give loving consideration to 'A longlegs, a moth and a dumbledore' which enter on *An August Midnight* to join 'A sleepy fly, that rubs its hands' on Hardy's 'page'. To most of us an irritation, this is to Hardy something more significant:

'God's humblest, they!' I muse. Yet why?
They know Earth-secrets that know not I.

Even these are his guests, and the unfailing sympathy Hardy extends to all living creatures is exemplified here. But his concern with the minute did not lessen his sensitivity to great events. The loss of the *Titanic* moved him to a majestic, sombre poem, full of strange under-water imagery:

Over the mirrors meant
To glass the opulent
The sea-worm crawls—grotesque, slimed, dumb, indifferent.

The poem moves with a cold inevitability, matched by the slow beat of the verse, to its fore-doomed conclusion. It is, in a way, weirdly prophetic too, for in it Hardy attacks the illusion that man is master of his fate, an illusion the First World War was soon to destroy entirely. Despite the variety within this category, however, it is possible to think of Hardy's reflective poems in two main groups, as follows:

1. Poems about people, living or dead, whom Hardy knew or was influenced by in some way.

2. Poems having their origin in a consideration of some place remembered or revisited, or some object with strong associations for Hardy.

1. *Poems about people.* Perhaps no poet has ever paid finer tributes to those, living or dead, who have influenced him, than Hardy. He shows us Shakespeare's fellow-townsmen discussing his death in banal phrases; 'A worthy man and well-to-do' . . . 'I' faith, few knew him much here', and the Squire's wife, 'Ah, one of the tradesmen's sons, I now recall', snobbishly summing up. This dull but realistic chatter enables him to contrast the 'real' Shakespeare, by means of the still homely but vivid simile of some 'strange bright bird' which comes mysteriously to dwell among 'the barndoor brood'. So Shakespeare came into man's poesy, 'lodged there a radiant guest and sped forever thence'. Hardy's old friend and teacher, William Barnes, his early adviser, George Meredith, and Keats, whom he idolised—all inspire Hardy to write uncommonly well. There is a charming poem to Shelley's Skylark, delicate and fragrant as Shelley's own work. Gibbon, author of *The Decline and Fall of the Roman Empire*, whose sceptical brilliance and total dedication to the truth drew Hardy's admiration, is the subject of a poem Hardy wrote in Gibbon's old garden in Lausanne. His ghost returns to ask, 'How fares the truth now?' and to enquire whether there

> "Still rule those minds on earth
> At whom sage Milton's wormwood words were hurled:
> *'Truth like a bastard comes into the world*
> *Never without ill-fame to him who gives her birth'*?"

a deft condensation by Hardy of a much longer passage by Milton, and a reflection upon much of Hardy's own experience —he had only just been through the hullaballoo about *Jude the Obscure* at this time.

There are more personal poems, *To a Pet Cat, Wessex, the Dog to the Household*, and one, *To my Father's Violin*, is really a moving elegy on Hardy's father. There is deep sadness in the picture of the silent violin, which stands for Hardy's father's own silence and remoteness in those 'Mournful Meads' where 'No bowing wakes a congregation's wonder'.

In *Friends Beyond* the mood changes. These jingling vignettes of the Mellstock village-folk 'murmuring mildly' out of their graves slyly insinuate how little their earthy and earthly pre-occupations mattered against 'the morrow free of thought' where, 'ignoring all that haps beneath the moon', William Dewy, Tranter Reuben, Farmer Ledlow 'late at plough' sleep forever. It is a mellow poem, not without humour, contrasting sharply with a poem of dancing gaiety, *Regret not me*, in which Hardy exploits a timeless theme best summed up in Herrick's line, 'Gather ye Rosebuds while ye may'.

> Regret not me;
> Beneath the sunny tree
> I lie uncaring, slumbering peacefully.
>
> Again you will fare
> To cider-makings rare
> And junketings; but I shall not be there.
>
> Yet gaily sing
> Until the pewter ring
> Those songs we sang when we went gipsying.

Here there is 'nothing for tears'; only a masterly ease and grace upon which sadness lies lightly; and the rich detail of the rural scene, the joyful sights and sounds make the whole poem 'lightly dance' and the reader 'forget mischance'.

To the next poem to be considered we may apply Dr. Johnson's remark on Gray: 'Had he written a dozen poems such as this it would be as vain to praise as to blame him'. It's true that in *To An Unborn Pauper Child* Hardy isn't free from those tricks of style which some critics object to; our old friends the 'Doomsters' appear, for instance, with angular phrases like 'wombéd souls' and 'to theeward'. Yet here, in full flood, he rides majestically over such trivialities, forcing us indeed to accept them as inevitable and right. Always, with Hardy at his best, 'the style is the man himself', and this poem is, in any case, as much about Hardy as it is about the unborn child whom he addresses so softly:

> Breath not, hid Heart: cease silently,

he begins, because, as he puts it with sad resignation:

> Hopes dwindle; yea,
> Faiths waste away,
> Affections and enthusiasms numb;
> Thou canst not mend these things if thou dost come.

He wishes he could

> ... tell thee all I know
> And put it to thee: Wilt thou take Life so?

In answer to this question (which is in effect Hardy's own question, elsewhere expressed as a demand to know whether life is really 'A senseless school where we must give/Our lives that we may learn to live') comes the 'turn' of the poem, and here the whole of the last three stanzas must be quoted, for their slow cumulative movement has a good deal to do with the poem's total effect:

> Vain vow! No hint of mine may hence
> To theeward fly: to thy locked sense
>   Explain none can
>   Life's pending plan:
> Thou wilt thy ignorant entry make
> Though skies spout fire and blood and nations quake.
>
> Fain would I, dear, find some shut plot
> Of earth's wide wold for thee, where not
>   One tear, one qualm,
>   Should break the calm.
> But I am weak as thou and bare;
> No man can change the common lot to rare.
>
> Must come and bide. And such are we—
> Unreasoning, sanguine, visionary—
>   That I can hope
>   Health, love, friends, scope
> In full for thee; can dream thou'lt find
> Joys seldom yet attained by humankind!

It is hard to know where to begin commenting. First perhaps comes the skill with which the theme is developed, the to-and-fro movement of the ideas that keeps up the pressure on the reader's mind; just as if Hardy were thinking aloud, turning over first one idea and then another. Then comes the use of contrast: the 'violent' last line of stanza IV is set against the infinitely gentle beginning of stanza V. If only a dozen lines of Hardy's work were to be left to speak for Hardy the man and the poet, I should be tempted to choose these last two stanzas. No one could miss the sheer skill, here a matter of absolute bareness of phrasing, where he is speaking to the child. (In V all words but one are monosyllabic, and that one is indeed common enough.) The use of pauses to produce an effect of hesitation, as if not wanting to give pain, makes the truth, at last so hesitantly expressed, the more moving. This touching plainness and tenderness is set against the sudden flow of phrases (significantly more elaborate and intellectual) suggesting a happier future, which echo every reader's wish for the child, but which are balanced by Hardy's quiet return upon himself at the end. Yet it is the quality of the maker's mind which ultimately stamps this or any other poem with that durable beauty and power 'to tear the heart' that Pope spoke of. So Hardy believed, and so it is here, where an almost god-like compassion informs every line, and yet Hardy never allows the edge of his insight to be blunted by sentimentality. Just as Shakespeare, in Lear's words on the heath, gives us a universal vision of mankind assailed by misfortune:

Poor naked wretches, whereso'er ye be,
That bide the pelting of this pitiless storm,

so Hardy here gives us his vision of suffering humanity (for this child is surely 'Everyman'). Hardy certainly isn't 'unreasoning' or 'sanguine'. Yet perhaps he *is* visionary, since to me at least this poem suggests that for man to accept, as Hardy does here, with complete honesty and humility, his own infinite littleness and weakness, is a first condition of his attaining any improvement whatever. And if we are to ask by what means this improvement is to be obtained, it must surely be through the power of that love which is written all over the poem for anyone to see who has not closed his eyes to it. For I am at a loss to see how anyone could have called Hardy cynical in face of poems like this and *Surview*, where Hardy hears 'a cry from the green-grained sticks of the fire' and realises ' 'Twas my own voice talking from there to me'. Then quietly and insistently, using the timeless phrases of St. Paul's Epistle to the Corinthians, Hardy examines his own life and finds it wanting:

> *'You taught not that which you set about,'*
>   Said my own voice talking to me;
> *'That the greatest of things is Charity . . .'*
>   And the sticks burnt low, and the fire went out,
>   And my voice ceased talking to me.

Few poets, Christian or otherwise, have written more humbly than this, and there is no gainsaying the force or the sincerity of the conviction which Hardy reiterates in his prose *Apology* to *Late Lyrics and Earlier*—that the chief aim of man should be to ensure that 'pain shall be kept down to a minimum by loving-kindness'. Only in this way can we hope to 'change the common lot to rare' (when he says 'no man' can change it he means 'no individual', of course).

The same Shakespearean blend of pity and truth can be found in *Drummer Hodge*, one of a group prompted by the Boer War. This pictures an 'unknown soldier' thrown in 'to rest, uncoffined —just as found'. Here are no conventional heroics, none of Rupert Brooke's later attempts to cheer up the non-combatants at home by sentimental fictions like the 'corner of a foreign field/ That is forever England', or the notion that the dead will be 'A pulse in the eternal mind'. Yet somehow Hardy's last verse suggests in its very plainness and utter honesty far more of 'the pity of war, the pity war distilled':

> Yet portion of that unknown plain
>   Will Hodge for ever be;
> His homely Northern breast and brain
>   Grow to some Southern tree,

And strange-eyed constellations reign
His stars eternally.

DRUMMER HODGE

Here is that restraint which by saying little tells us much, a quality found in the famous Epitaph on the Spartan Dead at Thermopylae:

Go, passer-by, tell the Lacedaemonians
That we lie here obeying their orders.

There isn't any consolation, except perhaps the beauty of the poem, but there is a deep humanity at work, just as there is in that weird dream vision, *The Souls of the Slain*, where the dead, returning as 'spirits' to their homes find, some with joy, some with bitterness,

. . . that our glory
Weighs less in their thought
Than our old homely acts.

Hardy wrote other war poems, some conventionally patriotic, about the 1914–18 conflict, but only the famous *In the Time of the Breaking of Nations* needs mentioning. Here Hardy sets the momentary insanity of war against the time-scale of all human history:

Yonder a maid and her wight
Come whispering by:
War's annals will cloud into night
Ere their story die.

2. *Poems of place*. Next come those poems which have to do with what Hardy called his 'place-enthusiasms'. It is important here to stress that Hardy is not a Nature poet, picturing the country scene like, say, Wordsworth or John Clare, or his old friend William Barnes with his 'Sweet Bemmister, that bist abound/By green an' woody hills all round'. Description isn't a prime object with Hardy, and although there are a few poems that do superbly depict Wessex and other landscapes, these are generally incidentally and occasionally shown to us in phrases

like 'open drouthy downland thinly grazed' or the fine ringing line: 'O Epic-famed, God-haunted Central Sea' (for the Mediterranean), or similar hints which leave the reader to do most of the work. At least, this was true until he stopped writing novels, which perhaps absorbed this function of his genius. Afterwards there are more poems of place. *Satires of Circumstance* begins with *In Front of the Landscape*, a vision similar to the great panoramas in the novels.

> . . . And the coomb and the upland
>   Coppice-crowned,
> Ancient chalk-pit, milestone, rills in the grass-flat
>   Stroked by the light . . .

while others—*Wessex Heights* and *Beyond the Last Lamp*—give us glimpses of what Hardy could do by way of etching a scene in a few lines.

However, a distinction needs making here. When Hardy writes about places, his object isn't to depict them (or only rarely is it so). A revisitation or memory of a scene (or perhaps some familiar household object) simply serves as a starting point from which Hardy works through to meditate on the meaning of what he sees or recalls. Obviously this method results in a good few poems where the connection between the place observed and Hardy's thought is only fragmentary. What I call 'poems of place' are therefore only those where a sense of locality is so strong as to be a dominant influence, and, since this is a matter of emphasis, I shall only use the term cautiously. Where what is seen is more important than the idea it evokes, then the poem is one of place in my sense of the word.

Thus in one early poem the sense of locality is very strong. *Her Dilemma* (1866) begins:

> The two were silent in a sunless church,
> Whose mildewed walls, uneven paving-stones,
> And wasted carvings passed antique research;
> And nothing broke the clock's dull monotones.

This vignette, with so much of Hardy's own experience in it, is followed by:

> Leaning against a wormy poppy-head,
> So wan and worn that he could scarcely stand . . .

This demonstrates how much Hardy gains by giving 'a local habitation and a name' to his poems; here the decay and ruin all around echo the sickness of a man soon to die, and the 'wormy poppy-head' with its hints of sleep and drugs makes us sharply realise how brief human life is against the age-long, slow crumbling of the wooden pew-end carving. All this comes out in the weird, vivid illustration Hardy drew for this poem (see illustrations). But we must go on to *Moments of Vision*, the first collection of which the contents were mostly written *after* the novels (which this poem preceded), to find a whole string of lyrics displaying similar qualities. The titles—*The Runic Stone, Where They Lived, At Middle-Field Gate in February* (with its fogbound sodden landscape):

> While the fallow ploughland turned up nigh
> In raw rolls, clammy and clogging, lie.

The Head above the Fog, On Sturminster Footbridge—all begin with the close, loving delineation of some particular spot or object. One may note in passing that Hardy's sense of 'where it happened' is very strong, too, in the 1913 Love Poems, which are indeed quite unlike most other love poetry in that they don't take place in a geographical vacuum, so to speak.

A particularly fine poem, *He revisits his first school*, shows us Hardy as a child:

> Pink, tiny, crisp-curled,
> My pinions yet furled
> From the winds of the world.

when he 'conned/The grand Rule-of-Three/With the bent of a bee'. It has a delicacy and courtesy of manner (Hardy feels he 'ought to have gone as a ghost') and a gently witty ending where he hints that he may yet do so. But without the crystal-clear picture of the school as it was the poem wouldn't satisfy us.

Later collections, and notably *Human Shows* with its ten pages devoted to scenes of frost and snow, contain many fine poems of place. *Snow in the Suburbs*, with its delightful picture of the sparrow on which:

> A snow-lump thrice his own slight size
> [*falls*]
>   And overturns him
>   And near inurns him.

is famous, but not better than *Life and Death at Sunrise*, for example. Perhaps the best of its kind, however, is *The Later Autumn*, which provides a fine contrast with Keats's wonderful evocation in 'Season of mists and mellow fruitfulness' of fulness and ripeness. Hardy's swift withdrawal of all signs of life in the first verse, with its unusual irregular movement:

> Gone are the lovers, under the bush
>   Stretched at their ease;
>   Gone are the bees,
> Tangling themselves in your hair as they rush.

is set against the silence, the damp, misty stillness, of verses two and three:

> Toadsmeat is mangy, frosted, and sere;
>   Apples in grass
>   Crunch as we pass,
> And rot ere the men who make cyder appear.

The detail is all-important here. These, to the countryman, are the marks of the season, and Hardy is more precise than Keats in fact—though not, of course, better on that account.

Undoubtedly one of Hardy's finest poems, *The Five Students*, will both neatly conclude this grouping and lead us into the next. Here, set against five masterly miniature landscapes—like tiny wood-engravings only inches square, showing the year's progress from high summer to the dead point of winter—is a subtly varied refrain showing Time, the old Enemy, picking off the 'Five' one by one. This is a theme expressed, crudely, in the *Ten Little Nigger Boys*. But here the actual treatment is brilliant and felicitous in the extreme:

The sparrow dips in his wheel-rut bath,
    The sun grows passionate-eyed,
And boils the dew to smoke by the paddock-path
    As strenuously we stride—
Five of us; dark He, fair He, dark She, fair She, I,
    All beating by.

This poem must be read aloud; then Hardy's contrast of the tiny sparrow with the sun itself, the sheer vigour of the phrasing (in '*boils* the dew to *smoke*', 'passionate-eyed' and 'strenuously') and the contrast of the musing refrain become apparent, as does the 'lift' and the springing rhythm which suggest the optimism, the 'high-uplifted hearts' of the five students. In the last verse all has suffered a grim change:

    Icicles tag the church-aisle leads,
        The flag-rope gibbers hoarse,
    The home-bound foot-folk wrap their snow-flaked heads,
        Yet I still stalk the course—
    One of us. . . . Dark and fair He, dark and fair She, gone:
        The rest—anon.

Here is a death-cold landscape—made up, however, of a few details only. It is in the choice and disposition of phrases like 'icicles tag', 'gibbers hoarse', 'snow-flaked heads' that the effect lies. Here the rhythm is heavy and dragging. 'I still stalk the course' compels the reader to slow down and should be compared with 'strenuously we stride'. The poem falters at 'One of us. . . .' and then tails hollowly away into emptiness and despondency. The process is one described by Hardy elsewhere as follows:

    But Time, to make me grieve,
    Part steals, part lets abide;
    And shakes this fragile frame at eve
    With throbbings of noontide.

                                    I LOOK INTO MY GLASS

It is, in this poem, depicted by infinitely skilful gradations. Yet it could never have been written at all by anyone who was not affected by an overwhelming sense of the significance of time

65

recalled, of changing scenes and places and of the seasons' un-changing progress. For what is implied, though never stated, what gives the poem its ineffable sadness, is the certainty that though all the movements of the passing year will recur, the human actors have gone forever. Only the one remaining—Hardy—remembers them, and only his love gives them any kind of continuance. Yet, soon, like 'The rest—anon', he too will be unremembered.

LOVE POEMS

The last but one of the 'students' to go was Hardy's first wife, Emma Lavinia. (The poem recalls walks taken by her and her sister, with her brother-in-law and Hardy. Horace Moule, Hardy said, was the fifth, though he was never in Cornwall with them.) There are perhaps 100 poems written to or about Emma Lavinia. I shall not pretend to write of them dispassionately. Beyond any question Hardy's greatest achievement, nothing to touch them has been written by any other poet of this century apart from W. B. Yeats, and even he did not produce so large, so varied, so majestic a tribute to that force in human affairs which Dr. Johnson—the last man to be considered sentimental—called 'a passion which he who has never felt never was happy, and he who laughs at never deserves to feel; a passion which has caused the change of empires and the loss of worlds'.

Because Hardy's love poetry, which of course includes earlier poems not written to his wife (amongst them some certainly, some very probably, addressed to Tryphena Sparks), is clearly the ultimate touchstone of his poetic genius, I intend to consider it at some length. It can be said quite simply that Hardy writes almost exclusively of Love frustrated and Love lost. Still, there is an important reservation to be made, for Hardy's love poetry displays a progression from one way of treating frustration and loss to another, wiser and more gentle, approach. Since this develops more or less chronologically, I shall discuss the poems roughly in the order that they were written, so far as that admits of discovery, and divide them into groups under sub-headings.

1. *Early love poetry*. The first group of love poems was written

in London during 1862–7. They contain many 'keen lessons that love deceives', they tell us (rather too frequently) that 'joy lies slain', and the young poet professes the desire never again to experience 'the fatal thrilling/That devastates the love-lorn wooer's frame'. They have their moments, especially the sonnets, but Hardy is too vigorously engaged in booting Cupid about to be altogether convincing. The fury of rejection is what we see, the Byronic 'pageant of a bleeding heart', not the totally untheatrical anguish that came later, when perhaps 'the hot ado of fevered hopes' seemed to him, as it does to us, rather a hectic and hollow turn of phrase. It's true that Hardy doesn't himself say 'Love is lovelier/The more it shapes its moan in selfish-wise' (he unkindly ascribes it to a woman). But Hardy's touch was less sure in the 1860s than it later became. One can't suppose many women would care to be praised in these frigid, condescending phrases:

> 'O faultless is her dainty form,
>   And luminous her mind;
> She is the God-created norm
>   Of perfect womankind!'

THE WELL-BELOVED

—even though it is Venus with whom Hardy compares his 'queen'. At least this poem contains some hard thinking. In:

> 'Brides are not what they seem,
> Thou lovest what thou dreamest her.
> ·I am thy very dream!'

we have a premonitory glimpse of the conflict between 'appearance and reality' which was later to figure largely in Hardy's poems.

Hardy also attempted to write 'pure' lyrics (poems in which the 'music' was what mattered most). One, which it is difficult to date—the idea after all was to write a 'timeless' poem—is *I need not go*. This has a gentle, indeed almost off-hand, beauty, arising from its simple phrasing:

> I need not go
> Through sleet and snow

To where I know
She waits for me;
She will tarry me there
Till I find it fair.
And have time to spare
From company.

This is much more difficult to do than it looks. Everything is *implied*: Hardy's grief, the grave in winter, the finality of death. Hardy can't quite keep it up, unfortunately. The third verse is thin and padded out. I suspect that this poem was written 'in the air', so to speak, and that is why Hardy loses his way—he hasn't an actual person in mind. On the other hand, in 1867, an actual person, Tryphena Sparks, came into his life, and made an impact upon it of which the echoes can be detected in his work many years later.

2. *Poems to or about Tryphena.* It had better be said at once that, with one or two exceptions, few poems can *certainly* be ascribed to Hardy's five-year-long engagement to this beautiful, but ultimately fickle girl. Still it is clear that poems written during this period, whether directly concerned with her or not, bear the scars of what was obviously a tempestuous, passionate, and finally agonising relationship. For a start, Hardy moves away from that tendency towards an almost callous self-regard apparent in the earliest love poems, and reveals that capacity for seeing the woman's point of view which is evident in the novels. His acute 'sense of place' is also notable in the poem, *In a Eweleaze near Weatherbury.* This with its macabre picture of Time ('the little chisel of never-napping Time' is an image a 17th-century poet would have been proud of) was decidedly written, though later, about Tryphena, and so of course was the sad memorial poem, *Thoughts of Phena at news of her death,* in which Hardy mourns his 'lost prize' now dead:

Not a line of her writing have I,
Not a thread of her hair.

More profound and more characteristic, however, is *A Spot.* This isn't dated—but Hardy would not have wished to hurt his wife by so obviously marking out a past episode, and in fact only one or two poems *are* dated during the period he was engaged to Tryphena. (Hardy was in any case very reticent—he hesitated to publish the 1913 Love Poems about his wife because he thought they were 'too intimate'.) Still I think *A Spot* is very probably written out of his experience with Tryphena; viewed, however, from a distance of some years. For nearly all Hardy's best love poetry was written long after the events he relates in it. It is as if we were looking through the wrong end of a telescope—everything is remote, but also crystal clear, and this quality is at once apparent in *A Spot*. (The spot is quite possibly the 'Eweleaze near Weatherbury' again):

> In years defaced and lost,
> Two sat here, transport-tossed,
> Lit by a living love
> The wilted world knew nothing of:
> Scared momently
> By gaingivings, = [apprehensions]
> Then hoping things
> That could not be . . .

It is the old Enemy, Time, who has 'defaced' the years—which Hardy pictures like the leaves of a book—but disaster is spelt out in the youthful arrogance which 'wilted world' (the world has faded when opposed to their love) and 'transport-tossed' imply ('transport' is here used in the literal sense of 'taken out of oneself'). It may be that 'hoping things that could not be' refers to Hardy's contemplated marriage. But, here in any case, biography doesn't matter much. What is really remarkable is the wonderful economy, the bone-bare, yet enormously telling, statements of the second verse:

> Of love and us no trace
> Abides upon the place;
> The sun and shadows wheel,
> Season and season sereward steal;

The first two lines show a clear verbal link with *The End of the Episode*, one of Hardy's very finest love poems, later to be discussed, and suggest to me a close connection. Yet the expected dark conclusion doesn't come here. Hardy 'turns' the poem to produce a charming, Keats-like fancy that softens the bleakness of the first two verses. 'Shepherds' may 'catch a faery sound', he says:

> On sleepy noontides from the ground:
> 'O not again
> Till Earth outwears
> Shall love like theirs
> Suffuse this glen!'

3. *More love lyrics.* The next group we have to deal with is that which Hardy specifically entitled *More Love Lyrics* and placed together in *Time's Laughing Stock.* These are a mixed bag: in subject, treatment and date they vary widely and are obviously only lumped together for convenience. Generally speaking they are unhappy, but they are not so demonstrative and self-pitying as the earliest ones. They contain a number of poems which are more subtle and more perceptive than any Hardy had written before. Several deal with the theme of disillusion. In one, significantly dated 1869, Hardy's 'vision splendid' fades to a 'sample of earth's poor average kind'. In another, *Shut out that moon*, we are given a magically beautiful first three stanzas. How many would guess that this was Hardy at all?

> Close up the casement, draw the blind,
>   Shut out that stealing moon,
> She wears too much the guise she wore
>   Before our lutes were strewn
> With years-deep dust, and names we read
>   On a white stone were hewn.

It is more like Tennyson, and this is even more true of the second verse perhaps. But in the last, acrid alike in thought, wording and imagery, the whole poem flattens out into a grey reality:

> Within the common lamp-lit room
>   Prison my eyes and thought;
> Let dingy details crudely loom,

Mechanic speech be wrought:
Too fragrant was Life's early bloom,
Too tart the fruit it brought!

There is a good deal here that invites comment. Superficially this is a rejection of what is romantic in life—for all the first three verses are expressed as negatives. But the effect is the opposite of the declared intention, for surely we are moved to reject the instructions 'Close up', 'Shut out' and 'Stay in' by those very scenes to which they refer. This is, I think, a 'two-faced' poem. Hardy suggests that a commonplace approach to love (as set out in the last verse) won't work, that however much our reason may suggest that it is 'safest' to 'imprison' ourselves in what is 'common', 'crude', 'dingy', and 'mechanic'—and how effective these words are!—'passion' will have nothing to do with it. This clash of opposites, this tension between what is explicitly stated and what is implied, between the arithmetic of thought and the music of feeling, is a prime mover in much of Hardy's poetry, as we shall see. Obviously this poem, like others in the group, has biographical implications—it is dated 1904. Hardy's unhappy marriage is also plainly referred to in *The Division*. But there are clearly some poems that aren't personal in the strict sense, and Hardy scrutinises various aspects of love quite clinically, as in *The Conformers*, a malicious exposure of how 'night-screened, divine, stolen trysts of heretofore' lead inexorably to respectability and life as 'a worthy pair, who helped advance sound parish views'. The milk of Paradise has gone sour somewhere, we can see. *I say I'll seek her* is an exception, it is true; very much in the folk-song idiom it begins gaily, and goes on:

'The creaking hinge is oiled
  I have unbarred the backway
  But you tread not the trackway
And shall the thing be spoiled?'

This frank invitation is like that in Burns's *Whistle and I'll come to you*. But—and this is where Hardy introduces a different and

individual note—it is not accepted. 'Indecision' in the man inter-
venes and the woman is left to cry:

> 'Far cockcrows echo shrill,
> The shadows are abating,
> And I am waiting, waiting;
> But O, you tarry still!'

The poignancy of this poem, for all its grace and charm, gives it
an added depth which stems from the conviction that dogged
Hardy all his life—the conviction that 'the road not taken' might
have produced happiness. Hardy doesn't often preach 'Seize the
moment' but he does suggest, indirectly, that we are often apt to
regret that we did *not* do more than what we did. The metre of
I say I'll seek her side, incidentally, is exactly like that of *The End
of the Episode* which I now quote in full because, like all the best
of Hardy's poems—and it is one of the very best—there isn't a
single wasted word:

> Indulge no more may we
> In this sweet-bitter pastime:
> The love-light shines the last time
> Between you, Dear, and me.
>
> There shall remain no trace
> Of what so closely tied us,
> And blank as ere love eyed us
> Will be our meeting-place.
>
> The flowers and thymy air,
> Will they now miss our coming?
> The dumbles thin their humming
> To find we haunt not there?
>
> Though fervent was our vow,
> Though ruddily ran our pleasure,
> Bliss has fulfilled its measure,
> And sees its sentence now.
>
> Ache deep; but make no moans:
> Smile out; but stilly suffer:
> The paths of love are rougher
> Than thoroughfares of stones.

What can be said about this? First, I think it is probably Hardy's farewell to Tryphena, his considered, painful verdict on their love, now terminated by her rejection of him. It can hardly be addressed to his wife (their marriage was not an *episode*) and it is obvious that something has happened *suddenly* to sever this relationship. There is an absolute mastery of form, and the form is a dangerous one because the double-rhymes Hardy uses in the second and third lines of each verse are often used for comic purposes in English verse. Here there is no suspicion of a jingle; the effect is to tie each verse into a tight separate ball, almost a miniature poem that could stand alone. This links it with *I say I'll seek her side*—and even more closely with *A Spot*, in which 'Of love and us no trace abides upon the place' seems to be a 'pre-echo' of the second verse here, and the theme is almost identical, except for the conclusion. Notable here, however, for the first time, is the way in which gentleness of expression over-lies ruthless thinking. There isn't any comfort; one by one Hardy knocks down the pleasing fancies that might, in part, compensate or the loss (this is in total contrast to the end of *A Spot*). 'Time is up': neither the place, nor the flowers, the harmless 'dumbles' nor even the fervent vows of the lovers can prevail over that implacable enemy. Yet this is in no sense a cold poem, for all its iron honesty. It is, throughout, full of warmth, of the 'fervour' and 'bliss' which the fourth verse gives us. It may be, as Hardy puts it with such heroic plainness in the last verse, that: 'The paths of love are rougher/Than thoroughfares of stones.' Still the final feeling we are left with is one expressed by Hardy in another poem, *To meet or otherwise*, that:

> By briefest meeting something sure is won;
>   It will have been:
> Nor God nor Demon can undo the done.

Hardy re-enters the past with ecstasy while still able, with another part of his mind, to consider it dispassionately; and this blend of a warm heart and a cool head is what gives an added poignance, peculiarly his own, to Hardy's poetry. This is a great poem because of its honesty, its insight, its refusal to evade the unpleasant, and its magnificence of expression. Hardy often equalled it but never excelled it, and if it *is* about Tryphena then we can certainly say that her 'immortality' is assured. It is an eloquent testimony to Hardy that no word of rancour towards the woman creeps in here, or into any of his later love poems. Though he had more than most men to complain of, he never descended to self-pity in his poetry. Rather he is sharply self-critical. The last poem in *More Love Lyrics, He Abjures Love*, begins briskly enough:

> At last I put off love,
>   For twice ten years
> The daysman of my thought,
>   And hope, and doing . . .

It has left Hardy
>   . . . bare,
> And poor, and starved, and dry,
>   And fever-stricken.

So he will leave these 'fatuous fires'. Then characteristically, in the very act of rejecting Love's 'disquietings' once for all, Hardy seems to cry out for them in an ecstasy of longing:

> No more will now rate I
>   The common rare,
> The midnight drizzle dew,
>   The gray hour golden,
> The wind a yearning cry,
>   The faulty fair, . . .

It is no use. Whatever Hardy had discovered of the miseries of 'heart-enslavement', it is its 'glories' that still compel him, and the glib, slick ending of this poem doesn't convince. 'Love is', in his own words, 'a *great* thing', though it depends upon a web of chance and choice as fine as gossamer: though it may, and often does, end in darkness and despair, it is supremely worthwhile.

4. *Summary of the characteristics of Hardy's love poetry.* This is perhaps a good moment to pause and look at what we have seen

of Hardy's love poetry as a whole; to try to draw together the various strands in it. These are: the conflict between Time and Memory, the clash between what the heart feels and the intellect perceives, the sense of love as both infinitely valuable and infinitely precarious, the finely-held poise between a pervading tenderness and a ruthless honesty, with, finally, a sad acceptance of the gulf between love's appearance and its reality.

5. *The poems of 1912–13.* All these threads are drawn together in *Poems of 1912–1913*. To this title Hardy added these words from Virgil: 'Veteris vestigia flammae', which might be freely rendered as 'Last flickerings from a dying fire'. In essence these poems are the record of Hardy's haunting by two ghosts—one, the figure of remorse, the other, the spectre of lost love. After her death, he came across Emma's artless recollections of her childhood and first meeting with him. He looked again at the water-colour sketches they had made together forty-three years before, and reflected on the barrier that time and his wife's near insanity had thrown up between them—'that thwart thing', he calls it in the one poem where he directly refers to it. Out of this complex of grief and regret, old love remembered, old haunts revisited, and his own magical facility for re-entering the past, he created a series of poems which express, better than any others I have read, both the searing pain of loss, and the sudden ecstasy of recapturing happiness long gone out of mind. He was seventy-two. These poems are the product of half a century's unremitting toil at his chosen art. He once wrote:

> Gaunt age is as some grey, upstanding beak
> Chafed by the billows of a northern shore
> And facing friendless cold calamity.
>
> THOUGHTS FROM SOPHOCLES

It is as if, from such a grim mountain as this, some long-dammed-up spring were to burst out, full of force and beauty, to turn the parched and rocky hillside green again. For who, even in the first flush of admiration, could write more splendidly than this of the country of romance:

Yes, I companion him to places
  Only dreamers know,
Where the shy hares print long paces,
  Where the night rooks go;

THE HAUNTER

or describe more delicately than this the 'swan-necked one':

With cheeks whose airy flush outbid
Fresh fruit in bloom, and free of fear,
She cantered down, as if she must fall . . .?

PLACES

But these poems do much more than evoke Emma as she was,
with her '. . . nut-coloured hair/And gray eyes and rose-flush
coming and going'. They summon up, in loving detail, the past
itself, its lost landscapes—'beetling Beeny crest', 'thin Vallency's
river', 'Where we made the fire/In the summer time'—and the
incidents connected with these places:

. . . she often would gaze
At Dundagel's famed head,
While the dipping blaze
Dyed her face fire-red.

I FOUND HER OUT THERE

and so sharply does Hardy experience them that he even doubts
their reality. 'Could this ever have happened?' he asks.

Does there even a place like Saint-Juliot exist. . . .
Or Beeny, or Bos with its flounce flinging mist?

APPROACH TO READING THE 1913 POEMS

There is much to say then, and certainly not room to say it all.
We shall probably get most out of these poems if we read them
in the light of the ideas and themes which, we have already
noticed, often recur in Hardy's poetry, and are here entwined in
nearly all the poems. The first poem, called *The Going*, begins
in an easy, almost conversational style which masks inner tor-
ment under everyday phrases:

Why did you give no hint that night . . .

Hardy asks his dead wife, that:

You would close your term here, up and be gone . . .

It is almost casual, until the sudden change of tone in:

> . . . gone
> Where I could not follow
> With wing of swallow
> To gain one glimpse of you ever anon!

reveals the rawness of the wound. The next verse begins in
tenderness:

> Never to bid good-bye,
> Or lip me the softest call,

and turns to self-reproach:

> . . . while I
> Saw morning harden upon the wall,
> Unmoved, unknowing
> That your great going
> Had place that moment, and altered all.

Here is that sense of insecurity, of love balanced on a knife-edge
already remarked on, and there follows the first hint of the
'haunting' theme:

> Why do you make me leave the house
> And think for a breath it is you I see?

But this is felt only momentarily, and how well 'for a breath'
conveys this fragility. The truth is that the

> . . . darkening dankness
> The yawning blankness . . .

'sickens' Hardy. He escapes in the next verse into an insecure
happiness, that moment 'While Life unrolled us its very best'.
Then regret and tenderness impel him to ask, uselessly, why they
had not striven 'to seek That time's renewal' in 'this bright
spring weather'. But it isn't in Hardy's nature to evade the issue

for long, which is precisely why he is so often heart-rending. His firm sense of what is ousts his attachment to what might have been, in his mind, and the last verse sinks us into despairing reality with its terrible broken phrases, its groping movement, its utter hopelessness, its image of himself as a broken puppet:

> Well, well! All's past amend,
> Unchangeable. It must go.
> I seem but a dead man held on end
> To sink down soon . . . O you could not know
> That such swift fleeing
> No soul foreseeing—
> Not even I—would undo me so!

Hardy isn't trying to write a 'beautiful' poem here. On the contrary this is how we speak when grief has stripped us naked of pretence. Yet only a great poet could have turned this disjointed fumbling into poetry at all.

THE 'FALSE DAWN' THEME

An escape from darkness into a false dawn of feeling and memory, only to fall back into an even deeper abyss of desolation, is a pattern which several poems in this group repeat. In *Your Last Drive* it is given an everyday context, and cast as a dialogue in which Hardy's 'dear ghost' herself points out the futility of 'visits' to her grave. The last verse begins with infinite tenderness:

> True: never you'll know. And you will not mind.
> But shall I then slight you because of such?
> Dear ghost, in the past did you ever find
> The thought 'What profit,' move me much?

But even as he is drawn into this 'conversation' he realises that it is all illusion. He has, momentarily, defied Time and intellect:

> Yet abides the fact, indeed, the same,—
> You are past love, praise, indifference, blame.

It is bleak, but we recognise its truth and are moved by it.

Much more simple, and perhaps tenderest of all these poems, is *Rain on a Grave*, speaking of Emma as:

> One who to shelter
> Her delicate head
> Would quicken and quicken
> Each tentative tread . . .

She is walking in the summer landscape of Cornwall, seen briefly here:

> When thunder-clouds thicken
> And birds close their bills.

But now that instant is gone, Memory and Love are powerless to protect her:

> Clouds spout upon her
> Their waters amain
> In ruthless disdain—

Cold, hard words; and 'arrows of rain' suggest that the elements are actuated by a personal hatred. Yet the ending is one of gentle resignation and recollection (Emma had loved daisies):

> Soon will be growing
>   Green blades from her mound,
> And daisies be showing
>   Like stars on the ground,
> Till she form part of them—
> Ay—the sweet heart of them,
> Loved beyond measure
> With a child's pleasure
>   All her life's round.

THE THEME OF LOVE'S FRAGILITY

Equally delicate and musical, speaking of love as something fragile and yet priceless, is *I Found Her Out There*. Here the heart rather than the mind is engaged, for there is much variety even in as closely linked a series as this. So in *Lament* Hardy lightly calls up his wife's delight in ordinary pleasures:

How she would have loved
A party to-day! . . .

or:

> . . . sought
> With a child's eager glance
> The shy snowdrops . . .

Yet as each verse dances gaily along it is suddenly checked by the harsh monosyllable 'But', followed by a tolling refrain (varied each time):

> She is shut, she is shut
> From the cheer of them, dead
> To all done and said
> In her yew-arched bed.

Memory opens the door, Truth closes it again, and the flat, dull beat of the refrain contrasts painfully with the eager haste of the verses.

THE GHOST THEME

In *The Haunter* the ghost theme is made more explicit, and I can't help feeling that Hardy had *The Unquiet Grave* in mind here—a ballad he certainly knew of, which contains these lines:

> The twelve-month and a day being up
> The dead begins to speak.

and is written in an almost identical metre. *The Haunter* is a strange, wistful poem, returning to an idea of Hardy's I have already mentioned, that the dead live on as long as we hold them in memory:

> If he but sigh since my loss befell him
> Straight to his side I go.

It is less sad, more fanciful, than most of the others, but Hardy's sureness of touch saves it from mawkishness, for the ghost, though she follows him:

> Into old aisles where the past is all to him . . .

80

(which might be a description of these poems), must remain:

> Always lacking the power to call to him,
>   Near as I reach thereto!

If the dead had in fact spoken directly, the illusion—for it is clearly no more—would be destroyed.

VARIOUS THEMES DRAWN TOGETHER

One of the most splendid and explicit statements of the various themes I have dwelt on is to be found in *At Castle Boterel*. With that 'hawk's eye' of his, Hardy looks down on an ordinary day 'in dry March weather', where he sees: 'Myself and a girlish form . . . alighted/To ease the sturdy pony's load.' He slowly moves closer to the distant figures—a favourite device in his novels—and so moves closer to the moment:

> Something that life will not be balked of
>   Without rude reason till hope is dead,
>   And feeling fled.

Here the conflict between head and heart is underlined. He goes on:

> It filled but a minute. But was there ever
>   A time of such quality, since or before,
> In that hill's story? To one mind never, . . .

This is a new idea, a new defiance of Time—that the *quality* of the moment is immortal. To 'Time's unflinching rigour' (the old Enemy appears undisguised in Verse 5) Hardy opposes simply this: '. . . that we two passed!' In a sense, nothing else exists, and the 'primaeval rocks' that 'border' the road in their ageless confrontation of the 'transitory' only serve to sharpen the impact of Hardy's challenge. Yet it is true for Hardy only— and, as he realises this, the moment fades: 'I look and see it there, shrinking, shrinking', and the poem dies away into a quiet resignation:

... for my sand is sinking
And I shall traverse old love's domain
Never again.

This is Hardy's most defiant poem. *Beeny Cliff*, already discussed, is his most opulent. Against its blazing phrases should be set *During Wind and Rain*, Hardy's most glacial verses. Here Hardy sees Emma as a child with her family in a series of gay scenes, each shattered by the intrusive, tormented refrain. Above the cheerful songs by candlelight Hardy hears, and cannot shut his ears:

Ah, no; the years O!
How the sick leaves reel down in throngs!

(and the choice of words in the last line is superb—suggesting confusion, drunkenness, perhaps death itself). In the beautiful garden: '... the rotten rose is ript from the wall.' Blake's 'invisible worm'—perhaps here the family's heredity, their tendency to madness—is in the poem. The triumph of Time is complete, the past itself is seen to contain the seeds of despair and death. The desolation is absolute, yet the poem has a tragic beauty which is summed up in the last marvellous line (itself almost a poem, so full is it of implication):

Down their carved names the rain-drop ploughs.

THE PAST RECAPTURED

Against this icy honesty may be set *Under The Waterfall* with its vivid evocation of all the warmth, colour and beauty of that high summer when the lovers:

Walked under a sky
Of blue with a leaf-wove awning of green,
In the burn of August, to paint the scene.

They picnicked by the waterfall, dropped a glass in it, and tried in vain to pull it out. Hardy painted the scene (see illustrations), and there is something curiously moving in the contrast between the rather clumsy sketch, precise but amateurish, and the commanding sweep of the poem, which seems mostly pictorial but conveys subtly and indirectly both the 'sweet, sharp sense of a

fugitive day'—the words 'sharp', 'sweet' and 'fugitive' tell us a
great deal about this and other poems—and the sense of the past
'crystallised', as it were, here at its strongest, and awakened, says
Hardy:

> Whenever I plunge my arm, like this,
> In a basin of water, I never miss . . .

so that 'The basin seems the pool'. The balance is held beautifully
between sadness and delight. For though the 'runlet' 'never
ceases' but (like Time):

> With a hollow boiling voice it speaks
> And has spoken since hills were turfless peaks.

and though the glass is still there 'jammed darkly', its smooth-
ness is now 'opalised' and like the moment itself (which perhaps
it stands for) it 'slipped and sank and was past recall'. But only
if one has lost the key, Hardy suggests, for here Memory defeats
Time, the heart is stronger than the head, the 'sense of that time'
is preserved, indestructible, in the glass. For the final statement of
the poem is this:

> By night, by day, when it shines or lours,
> There lies intact that chalice of ours,
> And its presence adds to the rhyme of love
> Persistently sung by the fall above.
> No lip has touched it since his and mine
> In turns therefrom sipped lovers' wine.

The 'glass' has become a 'chalice'—a magical cup and a symbol
of love itself which, like the song of the waterfall, is unending.
'Though lovers be lost, love shall not', as Dylan Thomas has
put it.

HARDY'S GREATEST ACHIEVEMENT
It is difficult to speak at all soberly of what, to me, are Hardy's
two greatest poems—*The Voice* and *After a Journey*. Both are
records of Hardy's feelings about his 'voiceless ghost', his 'woman

much missed', drawing him into the scenes of the past 'when our day was fair', 'the *then* fair hour'. It is with a shock of recognition that he 'sees' her in *The Voice*:

> . . . yes, as I knew you then,
> Even to the original air-blue gown!

But even as he invents the charming epithet 'air-blue', so suggestive of lightness and summery weather, the thought strikes him like a blow that this is only an illusion, the landscape changes to that of the present, the 'wet mead', the ghost dissolves to 'wan wistlessness', the pace of the verse slows, becomes halting, and the last stanza—perhaps the most desolate in English —perfectly conveys Hardy's final despair:

> Thus I; faltering forward,
> Leaves around me falling,
> Wind oozing thin through the thorn from norward,
> And the woman calling.

Though devoid of self-pity, it is almost unbearable in its hopelessness.

ANALYSIS OF 'AFTER A JOURNEY'

Finally, *After a Journey*, of which I quote the whole:

> Hereto I come to view a voiceless ghost;
> Whither, O whither will its whim now draw me?
> Up the cliff, down, till I'm lonely, lost,
> And the unseen waters' ejaculations awe me.
> Where you will next be there's no knowing,
> Facing round about me everywhere,
> With your nut-coloured hair,
> And gray eyes, and rose-flush coming and going..
>
> Yes: I have re-entered your olden haunts at last;
> Through the years, through the dead scenes I have tracked you;
> What have you now found to say of our past—
> Scanned across the dark space wherein I have lacked you?
> Summer gave us sweets, but autumn wrought division?
> Things were not lastly as firstly well
> With us twain, you tell?
> But all's closed now, despite Time's derision.

I see what you are doing: you are leading me on
    To the spots we knew when we haunted here together,
The waterfall, above which the mist-bow shone
    At the then fair hour in the then fair weather,
And the cave just under, with a voice still so hollow
    That it seems to call out to me from forty years ago,
        When you were all aglow,
And not the thin ghost that I now frailly follow!

Ignorant of what there is flitting here to see,
    The waked birds preen and the seals flop lazily;
Soon you will have, Dear, to vanish from me,
    For the stars close their shutters and the dawn whitens hazily.
Trust me, I mind not, though Life lours,
    The bringing me here; nay, bring me here again!
        I am just the same as when
Our days were a joy, and our paths through flowers.

All that has been said already about Hardy's poetry can be said
again about this magnificent lyric. First there is the mastery, the
assured ease with which what amounts to an extended conversation is handled. The 'voiceless ghost' obviously cannot
speak, yet Hardy with great subtlety contrives to speak for her;
the questions and answers are all implied. Even so there is no
sense of contrivance. In what could easily be a difficult or em-
barrassing theme, Hardy's restraint and impeccable taste sustain
him. Never once do we feel a slip into sentimentality, yet always
the verse is full of the deepest feeling, and this perfect balance is
maintained to the end.

The hesitance and wistfulness of the first verse are conveyed
by its soft sounds and irregular movement, the strangeness by
one splendid line—'The unseen waters' ejaculations awe me'—
and here the typically angular word 'ejaculations' is exactly right.
The sense of bewilderment, of puzzled groping, is resolved into a
clear and lovely picture of Emma, who appears throughout the
poem both as a person and, I think, as a goddess, representing a
now unattainable ideal, perhaps Love herself.

The warmth of the last line is set aside by the darker questionings of verse two, with its long, dragging movement. Here the

reiteration—'years', 'dead scenes', 'dark space'—serves to tell of Hardy's weariness and misery. These questions, so gentle, so lacking in self-justification, bring him face to face with Time, the arch-enemy, seen here deriding the lovers, and the verse ends harshly on this note. Memory replies by calling up the past, and in the wonderful third verse 'everything glows with a gleam', to borrow Hardy's own phrase. Here too is that sense of poignant fragility which plays so great a part in the love poetry: 'At the *then* fair hour in the *then* fair weather', Hardy writes, with what would be clumsy insistence if it did not so intensely convey his impassioned recollection that those minutes *were* enchanted. But all the warmth and light, now at their height, are extinguished in one stroke by the hollow last line. Hardy's age, the futility of his quest, the frailty of his vision are all at once renewed. Cold intellect strikes the warm heart dumb.

Even in the last verse, full as it is of natural beauty (significantly pictured just before dawn), there is no evasion. It is, Hardy knows, only in his own mind that the 'ghost' exists. With daylight, and when 'Life lours', she will vanish. But in these wonderful lines with their solemn music, their glowing contrasted images of night and day, their intimacy and affectionate humour (seen in 'seals flop lazily' and 'stars close their shutters'), it is not what is said that matters. Rather the old adversaries, Time, Reason and Truth of Fact, are all confounded, not by argument but by the sheer force of his conviction. So passionately does Hardy convey his vision that we accept what he defiantly asserts. However much we deny it with our heads, yet we assent with our hearts to another kind of truth—Hardy's:

> I am just the same as when
> Our days were a joy, and our paths through flowers.

Here, as in Donne's great line, Love 'Truly keeps his first, last, everlasting day'; and for us, as for Hardy:

> Time touches her not,
> But she still rides gaily
> In his rapt thought
> On that shagged and shaly

Atlantic spot,
And as when first eyed
Draws rein and sings to the swing of the tide.

THE PHANTOM HORSEWOMAN

For Hardy's poetry is rather like an oak; seen close, it will perhaps appear gnarled and earthbound, lacking in grace and beauty, but the flaws themselves arise from the massive strength and enduring vigour of the tree, and we lose sight of them in contemplating the splendour of the whole achievement; an achievement rooted in truth, wisdom and humility; a vision that, when others looked away, 'saw life steadily and saw it whole'.

4

The Novels

[He] in his own weak person if he can
Must suffer dully all the wrongs of man.

(W. H. AUDEN ON THE NOVELIST.)

HARDY'S IDEA OF THE NOVEL

I am going to begin by quoting and discussing Hardy's own remarks on the Novel generally, and particularly those which relate to *writing* novels, because, whenever we can manage it, we should endeavour to judge a man's achievement by what he was trying to do. As that great critic, George Saintsbury, put it, 'A is not bad because it is not B'. Hardy is very much an original; not at all like the run of other novelists, even good ones. Consequently many people, having been told that he is 'a great novelist', come to him expecting not only perfection but also work recognisably like what they have been used to. When, after an hour's reading, they find not only imperfections but also a good deal that is totally unfamiliar, they are put off—sometimes for life. One way of guarding against this danger is to see what Hardy's *intentions* were. He didn't always come up to them, it is true—probably no author ever has—but they give a much better touchstone of his true worth than any hazy 'definition' of 'a great novel', and enable us besides to counter T. S. Eliot's uncharacteristically wild charge that 'Hardy wrote for the sake of self-expression . . . and the self which he had to express does not strike me as particularly wholesome or edifying'.

First of all comes Hardy's comment on the 'real if unavowed purpose of fiction', which is, he says, 'to give pleasure by gratifying the love of the uncommon in human experience'. 'Pleasure' as Hardy uses it here doesn't just mean 'fun' of course: in this sense it includes both what we get out of *King Lear* and out of reading, say, *Lucky Jim*. What Hardy is concerned to stress is that 'telling a story' (preferably with a good many surprises) is an essential ingredient of any novel, and the fact is that, despite several attempts to avoid it altogether, virtually all novels do tell a story, and the wish to know 'what happens next' is found in all readers to some degree.

This wish was particularly strong in Hardy's reading public (see Chapter 2), so that since Hardy was, as he said, 'a working novelist', he was bound to try to satisfy it. He was in fact an excellent story-teller in the sense that his original ideas were good. Nearly all his novels display a clear, strong narrative seam, like the stories in the old tales and ballads he was so fond of. But this wasn't enough in itself. He was also expected, and did his best, to provide more elaborate 'plot-interest'. The difference may be illustrated in *Under the Greenwood Tree*, where the story is simply that Dick Dewy meets Fancy Day, falls in love with her, and eventually marries her. In the word 'eventually' lies the germ of the plot, for Hardy can't let the lovers marry straight away, just as Shakespeare can't allow Hamlet to kill the King in Act I. The element of suspense must be introduced; the 'Will she, won't she?' question raised, which makes us want to go on reading. In *Under the Greenwood Tree* Hardy only needs the Mellstock Choir and a bit of mild flirtation on Fancy's part to do the trick very neatly. But—because he simply wasn't interested in this particular technique of spinning a convincing web from action, cause, effect, coincidence, truth and falsehood—Hardy's plots are seldom the most satisfying part of his novels. He would probably have agreed with Trollope that: 'Plot is the most insignificant part of a tale . . . [only] a vehicle . . . and when you have a vehicle without the passengers . . . [it is] but a wooden show.' Hardy tends to provide us with fascinating 'passengers' in a very ramshackle 'vehicle'; indeed, he gives the game away himself when he observes: 'Human nature must never be abnormal' which is introducing incredibility. The uncommonness must be the event, not the characters.' Generally speaking (there are some glaring exceptions) Hardy's human beings—his characters —*are* credible. The same can't be said of the 'events'. Though he knew that 'the writer's art lies in shaping that uncommonness and disguising its unlikelihood, if it be unlikely', he didn't always bother about disguising it very thoroughly. Indeed, as he revealingly admits elsewhere, 'it is not improbabilities of incident' that matter. This attitude was partly owing to serial publication: he complained that he had been obliged to put too much 'incident' in *The Mayor of Casterbridge*. But it was partly due to disinclination. He brings about the, admittedly moving, climax of *A Pair of Blue Eyes* as follows. Knight, who is a London journalist and a man about town, having—incredibly— failed to hear of what must have been a large society wedding between Elfride (whom he loves) and Lord Luxullian, discovers it only by accidentally seeing her coffin-plate in a blacksmith's shop where he is sheltering from the rain with his rival, who has conveniently travelled down on the *same train* as Knight (and the coffin) to see Elfride, similarly unaware of her marriage! As here, Hardy's contrivances are often improperly exposed, to say the least of it.

There is indeed a good deal of evidence to suggest that, although Hardy's novels were nearly all written in the same convention as Fielding's or Dickens's—that is to say with external events playing a leading part in the unrolling of the plot—Hardy was increasingly dissatisfied with the novel of what he called 'physical sensationalism'. There is a particularly suggestive remark in his Journal for January 14, 1918 which shows where his real interests perhaps lay. He speculates on the 'possibility' of writing a 'psychical not physical novel' where 'the adventure is held to be of no intrinsic interest (i.e., not interesting in itself) . . . (but) the effect upon the faculties is the important matter'. He comes nearest to doing this in *Jude the Obscure*, which is, he says in the Introduction, primarily a record of the 'deadly war between flesh and spirit', adding (in a letter) that the novel was 'to show the contrast between the ideal life a man wished to lead, and the squalid life he was fated to lead'. In *Jude* 'consistency was not to be regarded as of the first moment'. (He means here consistency of plot, etc.) But when he was writing for his living he had to put a good deal of the 'merely physical' in his work, and so there is often a discernible tension between what he felt he owed his readers and what he owed himself. It's true he once said 'All I want is to be considered a good hand at a serial', but this is not to be taken too seriously. Still, it angered Hardy to be 'compelled to get novel padding from the (police) courts', as he records in his Journal.

Indeed the phrase 'novel padding' reveals that Hardy felt himself obliged to fill out his books with what he thought his readers wanted. This necessity meant that he also had to try to widen his 'range'. The idea of 'range' (which we get by analogy from, say, a camera lens, which has an effective range of from 5 to 30 feet) is of crucial importance in Hardy and needs defining. I can't do better than quote Robert Liddell in his excellent guide to the 'theory' of novel-writing (*A Treatise on the Novel*). 'Range', he says, 'means that part of the novelist's experience which he is able to use creatively.' All Hardy's collection of data from society parties did not enable him to write 'society conversation'. Consider this extract from *The Hand of Ethelberta*: ' "The action being like those trifling irregularities in art at its vigorous periods, which seemed designed to hide the unpleasant monotony of absolute symmetry", said Ladywell. "On the other hand, an affected want of training of that sort would be an even better disguise for an artful man than a perfectly impassible demeanour. He is two removes from discovery in a hidden scheme while a neutral face is only one", said Neigh. "You quite alarm me by these subtle theories", said Mr. Doncastle.' We sympathise with Mr. Doncastle in his perplexity; indeed, we share it. One really cannot accept that people ever talked like that. It's too stiff altogether, too contrived, and Hardy never learned how to make his 'society' characters speak convincingly. If we set against the *Ethelberta* extract a sample of Hardy at his best—a snatch of talk in *Far From the Madding Crowd*—we shall soon see where the difference lies. ' "Yes, she's very vain. 'Tis said that every night on going to bed she looks in the glass to put on her nightcap properly." "And her not a married woman. O, the world!" "And 'a can play the peanner, so 'tis said. Can play so clever that 'a can make a psalm tune sound as well as the merriest loose song a man can wish for." ' And this difference consists, of course, in what Hardy called 'the Illusion of truth', or, to put it in another way, the greater 'reality' of the second extract. But the word 'illusion' is important. For Hardy, in an essay (*The Science of Fiction*), derided the idea that any writer could ever be wholly realistic, 'an automatic reproducer of all impressions whatsoever'. 'If in the experience of his reason the novelist select or omit, with an eye to being more truthful than truth' he is, Hardy claims, a 'technicist', i.e. he 'uses the Daedalian faculty for selection and cunning manipulation'. In other words Hardy wouldn't have taken a tape-recorder into the 'Maltster's' gathering (in *Far From the Madding Crowd*), even if one had been invented. From his own experience he distilled the essence of such scenes—choosing, assembling, re-ordering and patterning them. In fact Hardy's instinctive opposition to 'Realism', to the attempt to provide a steaming, raw slice of life, sprang as much from his instinct as from his reason. For the 'natural magic' he talks of is precisely what he gives us when he is at his best. Unfortunately his own 'Daedalian faculty' (Daedalus was the master craftsman who made wings for his son, Icarus, in Greek mythology) is not always up to the strain he puts on it. Like Icarus he flies up towards the sun, the wings melt, and he falls down with a bump. For example in *A Laodicean*—admittedly his weakest novel—we are asked to believe in a tipsy Peeping Tom smacking his lips over a pink-flannel-clad girl gymnast. This isn't fundamentally improbable—but Hardy makes it seem so, somehow.

> Paula in a pink flannel costume was binding, wheeling and un-dulating in the air like a goldfish in a globe . . . she was irradiated with a warm light that was incarnadined by her pink doublet and hose. She only required a cloud to rest on . . . to be quite Olympian: save that in place of haughty effrontery there sat on her countenance only the healthful sprightliness of an English girl.

VII

To make someone a goldfish, an Elizabethan, 'Grace personified', an Olympian goddess and a healthy English girl all in one page is surely too much and I don't think, as some critics do, that this is a leg-pull. I think the truth is that Hardy himself was bored by these boring people. He couldn't be bothered to concentrate on them and simply used what came first to his mind for his descriptions. On the other hand, Troy's sword-play round Bathsheba (in *Far From the Madding Crowd*) is really a much more improbable event. Yet so charged is the whole scene with that electrical tension which Hardy could command when he was himself moved deeply, that we accept it completely:

> Beams of light caught from the low sun's rays, above, around, in front of her, well-nigh shut out earth and heaven—all emitted in the marvellous evolutions of Troy's reflecting blade, which seemed everywhere at once, yet nowhere specially. These circling gleams were accompanied by a keen rush that was almost whistling—also springing from all sides of her at once. In short, she was enclosed in a firmament of light and sharp hisses, resembling a skyful of meteors close at hand.
>
> XXVIII

If we look for one word to sum up this kind of writing, we shall almost inevitably be forced upon 'poetic': that is, 'having the qualities of poetry'. In this instance they are those of utter concentration on the thing considered, a most exacting choice of words to convey rapidity of movement and the element of risk (though this is done indirectly by massing over twenty words to suggest flashing or hissing) and the power to suggest more than is actually stated, for the sword is obviously both a threat and a lure to Bathsheba, offering, like Troy who wields it, light and freedom, gallantry and daring, and perhaps suggesting in its venomous hissing something of the snake-like treachery and slipperiness that this man is also to display.

Many novelists begin as poets, but Hardy never ceased to be one. Consider these lovely, slightly irregular, blank verse lines:

> Above the dark margin of the earth appeared
> Foreshores and promontories of coppery cloud,

Bounding a green and pellucid expanse
In the western sky:
Amaranthine glosses come over them then,
And the unresting world wheeled her round to
A contrasting prospect eastward, in the shape
Of indecisive and palpitating stars.
She gazed upon their silent throes amid
The shades of space but realised none at all.
Her troubled spirit was far away with Troy.

They will not be found in Hardy's *Collected Poems* because they are the conclusion to a chapter entitled 'Fury' in *Far From the Madding Crowd*, and Hardy wrote them as prose without line divisions. But in thinking of the sunset which is here so splendidly evoked, of Bathsheba's deep sadness after her encounter with Boldwood, and the way her mood and the skyscape mirror each other, Hardy has become so involved in the scene that he has actually broken into verse without realising it. It is unusual, of course, for him to carry his poetic impulse to the point where he actually writes in metre, but it remains true that these visionary flashes, these glittering and unforgettable moments, are what make Hardy a great novelist, and those novels where there are few such episodes have never been much read. He knew this himself. 'My art', he says, 'is to intensify the expression of things . . . so that the heart and inner meaning is made vividly visible'—a remark too seldom noticed, as is his revealing comment on Turner, 'The much decried, mad, late Turner rendering is now necessary to create my interest'. This tells us a good deal about Hardy's own descriptive techniques, for Turner's superb evocations of light in paintings like 'Rain, Steam and Speed' were not much liked at that time, not being sufficiently photographic for contemporary taste.

However much Hardy talks about craft, then, it is not as a craftsman novelist that he succeeds. It has been said that 'Consistency is the hobgoblin of little minds'. Hardy hadn't got a little mind, but he certainly could have done with a greater ration of consistency. Indeed there are times when one wishes that he had something of Anthony Trollope's workaday virtues, in particular his steady attention to what was probable, to lift him over the unavoidable explanations, continuations, routine conversations and so on, which were often stumbling blocks to him.

It was said earlier that Hardy's characters are generally credible and so they are. Henchard, for instance, in *The Mayor of Casterbridge*, is massively real. We know a good deal more about him than we do about many of our friends, and Hardy's sub-title, 'The Story of a Man of Character', is a just one. The suggestion has been made that character in a novel doesn't much matter anyway. 'All the writer need do is to provide bold out-lines and the reader will co-operate to persuade himself that he is in touch with real people.' Whether this is generally true or not (and I don't think it is) it certainly is not true of Hardy. As we have seen in his remarks on the desirability of 'psychical not physical novels', it was people who intrigued him. 'A Tragedy', he says, 'should arise from the gradual closing in of a situation that comes of ordinary human passions, prejudices and am-bitions;' and he says also, 'I am convinced that persons are successively various persons, according as each special strand in their characters is brought uppermost by circumstances'. All this is true of Henchard, and his character is exposed in intricate detail and in many different ways (which are more closely examined later). Yet although Hardy could see the necessity 'to avoid improbabilities of character', as he put it, the same diffi-culties arise here as with the plots—though far less frequently. Probably no novelist was ever equally concerned with all his characters, but few have treated those they do not care for as indifferently as Hardy. Certain people make an appeal to him, just as certain incidents do; he catches fire from a consideration of their particular fate; he visualises them intensely and they are charged with life at once. This has nothing much to do with their relative importance. The central triangle of *Tess of the D'Urber-villes* consists, besides Tess herself, of Alec D'Urberville and Angel Clare. Her are some samples of Alec's conversation on the first occasion we meet him. 'And so, my pretty girl, you've come on a friendly visit to us, as relations. Supposing we walk round the grounds to pass the time, my pretty coz.' We can almost see him slap his thigh with a riding-crop—and his final reflection after she is gone needs no comment. 'Well, I'm damned! What a funny thing! Ha, Ha, Ha! What a crumby girl!' Here is Sir Jasper, the villainous squire, twirling his moustache; we are in the world of Maria Marten; we almost expect the traditional 'Pretty and coy, yet she shall be mine' to follow this outburst. Alec D'Urberville is a stick and remains one throughout because Hardy can't or won't get 'inside' him. This is a grave defect and it cannot be denied that it appears with some frequency in Hardy's work, though in varying forms of course. But Hardy actually said of Tess, 'If I had known what a stir [it] was going to make, I should have tried to make it a better book', and there is much other evidence to show that he lacked that sharply self-critical faculty which is necessary to a novelist who wishes to avoid 'troughs' in his work. Lord David Cecil has very well argued the case that Hardy's weakness arises from his 'models'. These—Scott, Dickens, Fielding and Dumas—whom Hardy admired and emulated, were all notoriously unequal writers. Even so, as Cecil goes on to say (in his invaluable Hardy the Novelist), Hardy's real talent was much more like that of the Elizabethan dramatists than it was like that of his great contemporaries. Hardy hadn't much time for authors like Henry James and Robert Louis Stevenson, who made a fetish of style, and twittered away about Tess as follows: 'It is chockful of faults and falsity.' 'Oh yes, dear Louis, she is vile.'—while remaining on friendly terms with Hardy. It is not surprising he called them the 'Osric and Polonius of novelists' when he found out. Though he could see very well where James's talents lay, he remarks that, after reading one of his lesser novels, 'one feels inclined to be purposely careless in detail'. As we have seen, he *was* careless in detail over plot and character. His comments on style are as follows. 'The whole secret of a living style and the difference between it and a dead style lies in not having too much style—being a little careless, or rather, seeming to be here and there.' Undoubtedly this statement is true of Hardy's own practice, but there is also, one suspects, a little of self-defence in it. For Hardy often wrote in a hurry, and when later he heavily revised all his books for the Wessex Edition he was, to quote Weber, 'tireless in the attempt not only to correct faulty punctuation and grammar but also to strengthen diction, beautify rhythm, clarify thought and enrich the suggestive power of his lines'. This suggests (to me if not to Mr. Weber) that his remark to Hamilton Garland, an American visitor to Max Gate. . . . 'There isn't any technique about prose, is there? It just comes along of itself . . .' was something of a leg-pull. But certainly even with revision his novels are not free from stylistic faults any more than his poems are. It isn't worth going into too much detail here. One example of his reach-me-down style will do (from *The Hand of Ethelberta*):

> The sympathy of unlikeness might lead the scion of some family, hollow and fungous with antiquity and as yet unmarked by mésalliance, to be won over by her story; but the antipathy of resemblance would be ineradicable.
>
> XXV

This is both stiff and woolly. Hardy can also be unintentionally absurd, as in this passage from *A Laodicean* (my italics):

> The cheering message from Paula to Somerset sped through the loophole of Stancy Castle, over the trees, along the railway, under bridges, across four counties—from extreme antiquity of environment to sheer modernism—and finally landed itself on a table in Somerset's chambers *in the midst of a cloud of fog*. He read it, and in the moment of reaction from the depression of his past days, clapped his hands like a child.

He can be laboriously pedantic in his use of words too; 'But he could not help thinking of Elizabeth, and the quarter of the horizon in which she lived. Out of this it happened that the centrifugal tendency imparted by weariness of the world was counteracted by the centripetal influence of his love for his step-daughter' (*The Mayor of Casterbridge*). But, and it is an all-important qualification, Hardy's faults in his prose, like those in his poetry, arise from his originality. It is precisely because he wrote like no one else that he was able to achieve brief descriptions as memorable as this from *The Trumpet Major*:

97

Immediately before her was the large, smooth mill-pond, overfull, and intruding into the hedge and into the road. The water, with its flowing leaves and spots of froth, was stealing away like Time, under the dark arch, to tumble over the great, slimy wheel within.   XV

Just the two words 'like Time' open up a new perspective to us. Also at his command are splendid glowing pictures like this from *The Woodlanders*, where all the warmth, richness and colour combine to make of Giles a picture of the season itself: 'He looked and smelt like Autumn's very brother, his face being sunburnt to wheat colour, his eyes blue as cornflowers, his sleeves and leggings dyed with fruit stains, his hands clammy with the sweet juice of apples, his hat sprinkled with pips and everywhere about him that atmosphere of cider which at its first return each season has such an indescribable fascination for those who have been born and bred among the orchards.' Here every detail is telling.

He can be drily humorous, poking fun at the then growing vogue for old houses. 'The rambling and neglected dwelling had all the romantic excellencies and practical drawbacks which such mildewed places share in common with caves, mountains, wildernesses, glens and other homes of poesy that people of taste wish to live and die in' (*The Trumpet Major*). Or, more uproariously, he can produce jokes, mostly verbal (as here in *The Mayor of Casterbridge*), that are very funny indeed: 'True; your mother was a very good woman—I can mind her. She were rewarded by the Agricultural Society for having begot the greatest number of healthy children without parish assistance, and other virtuous marvels.'

You will look in vain for anything like these extracts anywhere else in Victorian fiction. For Hardy tore up the rule book and invented his own; which was in some ways a pity because the rules were often good and sensible enough. But scenes like this from *The Mayor of Casterbridge* do not come into being by accident:

At the town-pump there were gathered when he passed a few old inhabitants, who came there for water whenever they had, as at present, spare time to fetch it, because it was purer from that original fount than from their own wells. Mrs. Cuxsom, who had been standing there for an indefinite time with her pitcher, was describing the incidents of Mrs. Henchard's death, as she had learnt them from the nurse.

'And she was as white as marble-stone', said Mrs. Cuxsom. 'And likewise such a thoughtful woman too—ah, poor soul—that 'a minded every little thing that wanted tending. "Yes", says she, "when I'm gone, and my last breath's blowed, look in the top drawer o' the chest in the back room by the window, and you'll find all my coffin clothes; a piece of flannel—that's to put under me, and the little piece is to put under my head; and my new stockings for me feet—they are folded 'longside, and all my other things. And there's four ounce pennies, the heaviest I could find, a-tied up in bits of linen, for weights—two for my right eye and two for my left eye," she said. "And when you've used 'em, and my eyes don't open no more, bury the pennies, good souls, and don't ye go spending 'em, for I shouldn't like it. And open the windows as soon as I am carried out, and make it as cheerful as you can for Elizabeth-Jane." '

'Ah, poor heart!'

'Well, and Martha did it, and buried the ounce pennies in the garden. But if ye'll believe words, that man Christopher Coney went and dug 'em up, and spent 'em at the Three Mariners. "Faith", he said, "why should death rob life o' fourpence? Death's not of such good report that we should respect 'en to that extent," says he.'

'"Twas a cannibal deed,' deprecated the listeners.

' "Gad, then, I won't quite ha'e it", said Solomon Longways. "I say it to-day, and 'tis a Sunday morning, I wouldn't speak wrongfully for a zilver zixpence at such a time. I don't see noo harm in it. To respect the dead is sound doxology; and I wouldn't sell skellintons—leastways respectable skellintons—to be varnished for 'natomies, except I were out o' work. But money is scarce, and throats get dry. Why *should* death rob life o' fourpence? I say there was no treason in it."

'Well, poor soul; she's helpless to hinder that or anything now', answered Mother Cuxsom. 'And all her shining keys will be took from her, and her cupboards opened; and little things 'a didn't wish seen, anybody will see; and her wishes and ways will be as nothing!'

XVIII

A justly famous scene, this is often quoted as an example of Hardy at his peak. But normally only the last paragraph is given, and I think this is insufficient to show Hardy's wonderful grasp of structure and contrast. We should notice, first of all, the way in which (after concisely setting the scene) he begins and ends on the same note—Mother Cuxsom's strangely moving, almost biblical sentences. But Hardy doesn't overdo it; he makes these rhythmic, indeed poetic, cadences seem accidental and thus credible, by also giving Mother Cuxsom rough phrases like 'my last breath's blowed' and by the homely details, the dour earthiness, of the dead woman's instructions. Indeed it is all utterly convincing—and the fact that Mother Cuxsom is relating it makes it more so than if it had been a death-bed scene (Hardy incidentally nearly always avoids these). The tone of the extract then shifts from one kind of realism—a sad yet commonsensical facing up to the fact of death, where grief is genuine, though implied rather than uttered—to another, the dry, stubborn refusal to waste sentiment on what is beyond change. Dickens, great novelist though he was, could never have written, 'Why *should* death rob life o' fourpence?' But Hardy was particularly concerned, as he boldly claimed, 'to show the sorriness underlying the grandest things and the grandeur underlying the sorriest things', and this is precisely what he does here. The gentle crackle of humour which Solomon Longways's curious language stirs up is hushed by the return of the opening mood. We have seen death confronted with pity, courage, humour, even a kind of defiance—'Death's not of such good report that we should respect 'en to that extent'—and now at the last Mother Cuxsom sums it all up with her comments on the finality, the inevitability of death. The vigour of the language ' 'Twas a cannibal deed'; the dour honesty of 'except I were out o' work'; and the perfect aptness of Hardy's few adjectives, e.g. 'shining keys'—all contribute to make something entirely original and deeply moving out of a few moments' casual conversation among minor characters. Yet the author's eye is on eternity throughout, and it is just this universality of thought in a highly local setting which gives the passage its enduring power.

We begin to see why Hardy said of Henry James that 'his subjects are those one could be interested in when there is nothing larger to think of'. That is at once the root of Hardy's weakness and the core of his greatness. His conception of humanity involved in a tragic and generally futile struggle with fate overshadows all his later work, and when considerations of likelihood in plot or consistency in character threaten to interfere with this (as he thought it) inevitable process, Hardy generally ignores them or brushes them carelessly aside. Yet when wrought up to his highest pitch, so majestically does he write, so irresistible is the sweep of his creation, that in the end we yield to it. And this is the way to read Hardy—not quibbling over this or that petty infringement of credibility, but immersing ourselves in his work. There are two splendid lines of John Webster— next to Shakespeare the greatest 17th-century tragic dramatist (and quite as erratic a writer as Hardy)—which a character speaks (in *The White Devil*):

My soul like to a ship in a black storm
Is driven I know not whither . . .

Hardy's greatest novels are like that ship. We don't get, nor should we look for, a calm sea or a prosperous voyage. We must resign ourselves to being tossed about, to occasional sea-sickness, to shipwreck even. But the risk is worth taking. Other writers may give us security and comfort, and better navigation perhaps, but not a tenth of the exhilaration, the poetry, and the splendour of creation which Hardy offers us. Charles Lamb said of Coleridge that he was 'an archangel a little damaged'. The phrase may be applied with equal aptness to Hardy.

INDIVIDUAL NOVELS

The fact that a novel is not fully dealt with in what follows means that it is not, in my opinion, one of Hardy's best. This certainly does *not* mean that it is unreadable or not worth reading. For what it is worth I list these books (in ascending order of quality) below. They were written at various dates (given in brackets after each book) and it is only fair to point out that the first and worst on the list was dictated by Hardy when he was very ill indeed, in order to fulfil a contract.

A Laodicean (1896). Social comedy which starts well and then collapses in ruins.

The Well Beloved (1903). Expanded from an early idea; 'fantastic' theme too slight to sustain novel. (Man woos 'ideal woman' as mother, daughter and grand-daughter.)

The Hand of Ethelberta (1876). Hardy ill at ease 'below stairs and above stairs' in West End society. Poor 'stagey' dialogue. Has its moments, though.

Two on a Tower (1902). Obtuse young hero, keener on telescopes than on beautiful Viviette. Patchy 'society' parts, but moving love story when Hardy remembers to make lovers talk like human beings. Over-ingenious plot is a snag too.

Desperate Remedies (1871). Hardy's first novel, a thriller, chockful of coincidence and melodrama, but good lively reading, and (at times) looks forward to later Hardy style, especially in the rural passages. Hardy is doing his best to fill someone else's shoes and only narrowly failing.

A Pair of Blue Eyes (1873). Quantities of autobiography, beautiful description of Cornwall, potentially good tragi-comic theme. But too long (450 pages) for the interest to be maintained, and too patchy to merit detailed treatment here. Still it has lasting qualities, and is essential for anyone who develops a liking for Hardy, the man, though it will never be everyone's cup of tea.

The Trumpet Major (1880). Only lack of space precludes a more extended treatment of this historical novel, set in Trafalgar Year. It has a gaiety, sparkle and freshness which are all too rare in Hardy, and is often very funny in a rather Dickensian way. Hardy's fine descriptions of Overcombe Mill, that 'ancient manor-house' with its 'snowy dimity curtains', his splendid picture of H.M.S. *Victory* passing Portland Bill on her way to Trafalgar, his praise of Casterbridge strong beer, 'full in body, yet brisk as a volcano . . . luminous as an autumn sunset', all bear witness to his powerful feeling for the past. Though the end of the book is shadowed by the departure to his death in Spain of the noble and self-effacing John, who loses Anne, the heroine, to his scapegrace brother, Bob, the reader is not in the end left with a feeling of depression. Just as to the soldiers who once ate bunches of cherries at the Mill, that 'cheerful, careless half-hour ... returned like the scent of a flower to the memories of some of those who enjoyed it, even at a distance of many years after', so the sense of a past age more gentle and serene than our own is given off by Hardy's charming picture of life at Overcombe.

I am now going to write about the remaining seven novels in more detail, but I shall not, even so, attempt to discuss them all in full. Instead I intend to concentrate largely upon the *aspect* of Hardy's art which seems to me especially conspicuous in each of five novels in turn, and then to deal rather more fully with two acknowledged masterpieces, endeavouring to draw these threads together into some sort of pattern. A word of warning first—what follows will not make sense to anyone who hasn't *read* the novels in question; criticism is intended to be a walking-stick, not a wheel-chair.

'UNDER THE GREENWOOD TREE', AND THE HARDY WESSEX PEASANTRY
This was Hardy's first success, though not then a best seller, and it has always been one of his best loved books. Hardy called it 'a rural painting of the Dutch School', but I think it has more the quality of an English water-colour. It was the record of his youth, the book he wrote to please himself, to crystallise his memories while they were still fresh, and it is out of his heart's roots that the scene is drawn. 'Long looking, long loving, long desiring', wrote Walter de la Mare, 'these win at last to the inmost heart of a thing', and really that sums up what Hardy does here. He brings before us 'the inmost heart' of Mellstock (his own Stinsford), one tiny community, where the human characters are seen in their environment of work and play, 'in their habits as they lived', with the minimum necessary tinkering to shape a story, done tactfully and, as it were, in the background. Everyone is indeed pure Wessex, apart from Fancy Day; and her gradual reacceptance of the village, and its gentle pressure upon her to that end, is one of the themes of the book. Plot there is none, except the oldest of all. Dick Dewy meets

Fancy Day, the new schoolmistress and, as his father the tranter says, 'Dick's a lost man'. Fancy meets Mr. Maybold, the Rector, and is nearly lost to Dick. But for once in Hardy's books, innocence triumphs, and the gentle, shy and enchanted Dick is given his heart's desire. Yet Hardy can't avoid the note of sadness. Dick's joy is mirrored by Mr. Maybold's dismay, and there is a hint of tragedy, a foreshadowing of the bitter ironies that scar the later novels, in the way his disillusion is brought about by the happy confidences of Dick as they walk together. ' "Why, she's my sweetheart, and we are going to be married next Midsummer . . . the time will soon slip by", says Dick. "Yes, the time will soon slip along—Time glides away every day—yes." Maybold said these words but he had no idea what they were.'

Hardy has, though; it is by such words as these that he contrives to suggest the listless misery of love lost. Here is the same sharp insight into the torments of the human heart, the same wry acknowledgement that we often hurt people unknowingly, which is to characterise much of the later work.

Otherwise the book is not merely unclouded, but suffused with that soft, hazy glow so often to be found in the water-colours of men like Cox and De Wint or, Hardy's favourite, Turner. In their paintings the quality of the seasons, the shifting tints that mark one month from another, that distinguish sunshine from approaching rain, are lovingly delineated, and in Hardy the quality of living is as subtly conveyed, with an eye at once sharp to note detail and sympathetic to the victims of change. Hardy doesn't condemn, he doesn't get angry, he doesn't theorise or present a 'view of life', but rests content to observe, with love and irony, a scene where there is 'no enemy/But winter and rough weather', as in the song from which the title is drawn.

Hardy's opening is typically leisurely: the slow-paced movements of the eye across the landscape and the sudden closing-in on human figures is repeated time and again in later books. We ramble on to meet the true 'hero' of the book, the Mellstock choir, which will stand for that salient feature of all the novels (barring only *Tess* and *Jude*), Hardy's 'Wessex chorus'. 'Chorus' is a bit misleading as a description, because although these 'crusted characters' do at times comment on, and now and then even vaguely influence, the action of Hardy's books, this isn't their main purpose. They exist first of all in and for themselves, for the richness and sharpness of their own characters and talk, for the sake of the continuing, stable, ordinary life which they represent. They take existence as it comes, armed with a stoical, but not apathetic, readiness to bear pain and disappointment. They 'make shift and be satisfied'. In them common sense is elevated almost to a heroic virtue—whereas in many of Hardy's major characters it is notoriously lacking altogether. The choir, then, stands for much that mattered to Hardy and ought to matter to us.

First of all is the true feeling of community among them. Everyone belongs, even poor 'wambling' Walter Leaf, who 'never had no head never', as he admits. No one thinks any the worse of him because he will 'never be able to tell how many cuts d'take to sharpen a spar'. But, says Reuben, ' "I never see such a melancholy family . . . and as Leaf sings a very high treble, and we don't know what we should do without 'en for upper G, we'll let 'en come as a trate, poor feller" '. Here is a true and moving gentleness, people accept and make allowances for each other as an 'unimpassioned matter of parish history'. After the lovely vision of Fancy appears at the window on the night of the carol-singing. Leaf is even given a touch of the ethereal sadness Shakespeare gives to his clowns, when (after the others' commonplaces of admiration), ' "O such I never, never see", said Leaf fervently'.

The next thing to notice is the choir's blend of natural courtesy and naïve directness, which inevitably enables the vicar in the end to have his own way, though in that delicious scene where they beard him in his study, he is made to look rather foolish, albeit well-meaning. The way Hardy handles this confrontation is masterly. Firstly, the solemn, ponderous build-up to the event (Wessex like Sussex 'won't be druv')—its drily humorous discussion of what a vicar *should* be like—Mr. Grinham for example is praised because he was 'right sensible . . . never entered our door but once in his life' . . . 'very generous about Psalms and Hymns, saying, "Confound ye, blare and scrape what ye will but don't bother me" '. Then there is the quietly hilarious meeting itself, which is so satisfying as a whole that it would be a pity to quote from it. Afterwards the whole matter has to be weighed up, discursively and at length, of course. This is how things happen in a village, and gives Hardy opportunities to employ his genius for Wessex speech. It isn't just a matter of using 'Loamshire' dialect—Hardy hints at dialect only very occasionally in phrases like 'thirtingell as a chiel'. What he does convey marvellously is the *flavour* of the talk, its slow rhythms, its repetitions, its richness of allusion (often biblical) and similes, often vivid and apt. Indeed one has only to open *Under the Greenwood Tree* at random to hit upon phrases that remain in the mind for ever— as do some of Shakespeare's. Of watered cider, Spinks says, 'Such poor liquor do make a man's throat feel very melancholy—and is a disgrace to the name of stimmilent'. Surely this is Falstaff come to life again. Mrs. Brownjohn remarks of her fecund daughter: 'Five; they've buried three. Yes, five; and she not much more than a maid yet. She do know the multiplication table onmistakable well'—and we hear Juliet's nurse. The vigour that this speech can command is remarkable—when roused about music the elder Dewy can give us this fine tribute to it: 'Your brass-man is a rafting dog—well and good; your reed-man is a dab at stirring ye—well and good; your drum-man is a rare bowel-shaker—good again. But I don't care who hears me say it, nothing will spake to your heart wi' the sweetness o' the man of strings!'

There is humour too, sometimes dry and almost 'witty', as in: 'He can hold his tongue well. That man's dumbness is wonderful to listen to', and sometimes verbal: ' "She's a very good woman at bottom." "She's terrible deep then".' It can be in its own way philosophical, like the tranter's excuse for Farmer Shiner (who swears at the carol-singers—'Only a drop o' drink got into his head. . . . Man's well enough when he's in his religious frame. He's in his worldly frame now.' Hardy uses dialect very skilfully to show Fancy's real feeling for Dick when she finds him after he has stumped off in a huff because of her prolonged dress-making: 'O Dick, directly you were gone I thought I had offended you and I put down the dress: 'tisn't finished now, and I never will finish it, and I'll wear an old one Sunday.' In the chapter entitled 'Dick meets his father', the long, lazy and delightful conversation between father and son blends affection, homespun wisdom, humour and love all together.

The choir stands too for the capacity to enjoy life, something Hardy valued greatly. They seize the moment with a will when it offers. Their tremendous parties, the uproarious dances, the lusty singing, were all once seen by that frail child who fiddled the night away on just such occasions, and stored up for use the concentrated essence of it all, to be reproduced in passages like this: 'The room became to Dick like a picture in a dream; all that he could remember of it afterwards being the look of the fiddlers going to sleep, as humming-tops sleep, by increasing their motion and hum.' Those who have never experienced that feeling of intense, almost unreal delight are unlucky. No one has rendered it better than Hardy. Mrs. Penny's observation will sum up the attitude (a thoroughly sensible attitude it is too) which the choir share towards marriage: 'Well, 'tis humps and hollers with the best of us; but still and for all that, Dick and Fancy stand as fair a chance of having a bit of sunsheen as any married pair in the land.' She speaks for everyone, Hardy included, and the idyllic conclusion as the lovers ride 'over the hills and far away', and the nightingale sings, is typical of the book's spirit throughout. 'Tippiwit! swe-e-et! ki-ki-ki! Come hither, come hither, come hither! "O, 'tis the nightingale", murmured she, and thought of a secret she would never tell.' Across the lyric outpourings we seem to hear the faintly mocking note of the cuckoo—but the balance is perfectly held; this gentle twist does not, as has been suggested, darken the whole book. It just adds that spice of downrightness which the choir have provided throughout. They value the things Hardy thought valuable, and for Hardy goodness is perhaps a synthesis of those qualities the choir collectively possess—gentleness, kindness, loyalty—in a word, humanity.

'THE RETURN OF THE NATIVE', AND HARDY'S USE OF BACKGROUND

Perhaps the word 'background' as it is used here needs defining. By it I mean the non-human element in the Wessex novels which may include such things as the landscape, the weather, homes and their furniture, anything from the great thunderstorm in *Far From the Madding Crowd* to the leaky cider barrel in *Under the Greenwood Tree*. Many novelists do without much background—Jane Austen is an instance—while others only employ it spasmodically like Dickens in the eerie Essex marshland episode which opens *Great Expectations*. In Hardy, however, it is almost everywhere present, and generally of the first importance. To him figures are always seen against a landscape, and the nature of that landscape will always have some effect, often a crucial effect, on the human actors.

Hardy lived on the fringes of 'Egdon Heath', where *The Return of the Native* is set, and knew it like the back of his own hand. In no other book of his does the background figure so largely and so deliberately. Indeed it has often been maintained that the heath itself is a sort of character. I think this is an overstatement, but since roughly three-quarters of the book takes place in the open air and since Hardy insistently draws our attention both to the changing 'moods' of the heath, and to the reactions of the main characters towards it, it is plain that no better place to study his use of background is likely to be found.

I shall begin with two minor episodes, one an interior, one an exterior, since a good deal can be learnt of Hardy's technique by studying vignettes like these. The first is his description of the settle, during the party at the Yeobrights':

> At the other side of the chimney stood the settle, which is the necessary supplement to a fire so open that nothing less than a strong breeze will carry up the smoke. It is to the hearths of old-fashioned cavernous fireplaces what the east belt of trees is to the exposed country estate, or the north wall to the garden. Outside the settle candles gutter, locks of hair wave, young women shiver, and old

men sneeze. Inside is Paradise. Not a symptom of draught disturbs the air; the sitters' backs are as warm as their faces, and songs and old tales are drawn from the occupants by the comfortable heat, like fruit from melon plants in a frame.'

2, V

Hardy moves in from the implied coldness out of doors, through a craftily selected list of chilly discomforts, to a simple statement, 'Inside is Paradise', which he elaborates, stressing first the sheer physical pleasure, and then, with an unusual and wonderfully telling image of summer, the way in which one pleasure gives way to another. This in itself is highly satisfying: we can see and almost feel the precise degree of satisfaction that sitting in the settle brings. But the passage has a further purpose, and here we shall have to employ the word 'symbolic'. This is a useful critical term if used carefully and it means simply that an object or an incident 'stands for' something more than it directly states. Thus a weary shopper will use the phrase 'a nice cup of tea' to symbolise home, warmth, slippers, a fire, an armchair and so on; and a whole complex of pleasant ideas is crystallised in the 'symbol' of 'nice cup of tea'.

In Hardy's novel at this point the settle stands, I think, for the close, warm, unreflecting life of the Egdon Peasantry. Outside it are Clym and Eustacia, both for various reasons cut off from the snug, humdrum existence. Hardy immediately emphasises Clym's position by a long-winded description stressing his 'isolation' and perhaps rather spoiling the effect of the 'settle' as a symbol. This tendency to philosophise is very marked in *The Return of the Native*, and isn't one of its more successful features.

In the passage that follows Mrs. Yeobright, whose 'exertions, physical and emotional, had well-nigh prostrated her', lies down on the heath to rest. Her eyes fall first on a 'colony of ants' . . . 'where they toiled, a never-ending and heavy-laden throng'. Then 'she leant back':

> While she looked a heron arose on that side of the sky and flew on with his face towards the sun. He had come dripping wet from some pool in the valleys, and as he flew the edges and lining of his

109

wings, his thighs, and his breast were so caught by bright sunbeams that he appeared as if formed of burnished silver. Up in the zenith where he was seemed a free and happy place, away from all contact with the earthly ball to which she was pinioned, and she wished that she could arise uncrushed from its surface and fly as he flew then.

4, V

Here the symbolic intention is clear. The ants, far beneath her, stand for the apparently futile 'bustle' of earthly life. The splendid picture of the heron, always one of the most lovely and majestic of birds, is openly said to be an image of freedom and release from life itself. Yet, and this is important, both pictures are entirely accurate, quite unexaggerated, drawn with the sharply selective eye of a poet, no doubt, but drawn from life. It is when Hardy sticks most closely to strict truth of fact, as he does here, that he achieves his most moving effects. When he elaborates, when he underlines significances, and attaches human characteristics to the inhuman, he is generally not so successful; and it has to be admitted that he does it pretty frequently in *The Return of the Native*.

The opening chapter is famous for its evocation of Egdon. It contains numerous fine descriptive touches and flashes of perception, but it is a terrible mish-mash of good and bad all the same. When Hardy says that the heath is 'like man, slighted and enduring, and withal singularly colossal and mysterious in its swarthy monotony', he has at one stroke achieved a telling comparison, while 'The great inviolate place had an ancient permanence that the sea cannot claim' is as fine a sentence as Hardy ever wrote. But whenever Hardy turns away from the heath he knew so well to 'philosophise' in set 'essay' style, he at once becomes stodgy and pompous: 'Smiling champaigns of flowers and fruit . . . are permanently harmonious only with an existence of better reputation as to its issues than the present'. It is really difficult to see what this *means*, which is perhaps the gravest fault an author can commit. Clichés ('smiling champaigns') and jargon ('as to its issues') make matters worse. The general point then (which applies with special force to *The Return of the Native*) is that Hardy's use of background isn't uniformly excellent. Whenever he deliberately 'weights' the significance, there is danger of top-heaviness.

On the other hand consider this beautiful picture of sunset:

> The sun, resting on the horizon line, streamed across the ground from between copper-coloured and lilac clouds, stretched out in flats beneath a sky of pale soft green. All dark objects on the earth that lay towards the sun were overspread by a purple haze, against which groups of wailing gnats shone out, rising upwards and dancing about like sparks of fire.
>
> 3, IV

This closely resembles the passage from *Far From the Madding Crowd* quoted earlier (similarly falling into blank verse on several occasions). It makes beautiful play with gradations of light and colour, and it rises to an almost ecstatic conclusion. It conveys the still, almost trance-like quality of the 'green hour' to perfection. But it also suggests indirectly the feelings of Clym and Eustacia for each other—marking as it does the moment between their farewell and Clym's sudden proposal. The positioning of these background passages is always important. The lovers are themselves affected by the sunset—'Clym's feelings were high, the moment was passionate'. Yet Hardy is telling us a great deal more here about their love, suggesting not only the intensity but also the fragile nature of it, by his choice of background. It is an *exceptional* scene, quite untypical of the heath, and so Eustacia herself takes on an unreal quality, which disguises her essential shallowness.

As Eustacia walks away 'towards the sun' . . . 'wrapped in its luminous rays', it goes down, and 'as (Clym) watched, the dead flat of the scenery overpowered him'—its 'horizontality' became 'oppressive', which suggests that not only has light gone out of the sky but out of Clym's life too. Here Hardy gains enormously by subtly weaving human feelings and actions together with natural events, and here he nowhere overstresses the implications but allows them to emerge naturally.

There are of course many occasions when the Heath and its 'life' are used to affect the *action* of the novel. Much more important however than these, which the reader can readily pick out for himself, is the way in which all the major characters are related by temperament to the Heath. In one way or another their personalities derive from, or are reflected by, some aspect of the Heath itself. Eustacia hates it. ' 'Tis my curse, my shame, and will be my death', she says prophetically. It is a 'jail' to her, yet she is very like the Heath in her utter selfishness and in-difference to others. To her Thomasin is 'rightly punished' for coming between Eustacia and her 'inclination'. 'I have not much love for my fellow-creatures', she says. Nor has the Heath: it is, like her, 'indifferent', 'feline' and 'untamed'.

On the other hand, 'Take all the varying hates felt by Eustacia Vye towards the Heath, and translate them into loves, and you have the heart of Clym'. To him it is 'exhilarating, strengthening and soothing'—yet he too has some of its qualities, especially strangeness and remoteness. From the beginning he doesn't 'belong' with other people: he is idealistic, and thus, at times, inconsiderate. 'The eclipsed moonlight shines upon (Clym's) face with a strange foreign colour': he is out of place anywhere but on the Heath, and in the end Hardy identifies him with it by making him its itinerant preacher.

In complete contrast to these two is Thomasin: 'her fears of the place were rational, her dislikes reasonable'. Similarly Venn appears in some ways to be the spirit of the Heath itself and yet, with his quirky, vivid personality, warm humanity and quick-wittedness, is quite unlike it. He in fact *uses* the Heath, with respect and knowledge it is true, but it is to him no more than it is to Thomasin: he doesn't even mention it.

The Heath, then, is something which apart from its many particular functions in this book, has a larger significance as a symbol of inhumanity. It 'reduced to insignificance, by its seamed and antique features, the wildest turmoil of a single man'. The dual tragedy of Clym and Eustacia is that, in a way, they both attempt to live for themselves alone, without reference to others, though not from the same motives. But they cannot be like the Heath in its 'vast impassivity' and 'imperturbable indifference', and their attempts to escape the consequences of their common humanity fail because, just as Venn's and Wildeve's dice-game 'amid the motionless and uninhabited solitude . . . intruded . . . the rattle of dice, the exclamations of the reckless players', so Hardy suggests that the Heath will remain unchanged and unchangeable, indifferent as ever, when all these human antics, comical and tragic, are over.

'THE MAYOR OF CASTERBRIDGE', AND HARDY'S TREATMENT OF CHARACTER

Just before he wrote this novel, Hardy had read a book on 'Character' by Novalis, a German Romantic poet. One sentence in particular stuck in his mind and this Hardy quotes: 'Character is Fate'. In terms of Hardy's own book, then, Henchard's tragedy is (given the circumstances) an inevitable product of his own nature and not, as Henchard supposes, something inflicted on him by a 'sinister intelligence bent on punishing'. Shakespeare's 'As flies to wanton boys are we to the Gods,/They kill us for their sport' does not apply here, as it would for many of Hardy's characters. Henchard procures his own ruin. His attitude: 'I am to suffer, I perceive', stems, it is true, in part from a kind of fatalism, in part from imperfect self-knowledge. But Henchard simply isn't *capable* of understanding himself fully, and for this reason, I think, comparisons with Oedipus and Lear fail. I prefer to compare Henchard with Lemmy (in Steinbeck's *Of Mice and Men*), the giant whose unwieldy strength causes him to crush the puppies he loves in his great, clumsy hands. Hardy's genius has given us in Henchard a character essentially simple, superstitious, almost childlike, as much the slave of his emotions as a seven-year-old. In this lies his tragedy, but also the secret of his appeal to us. Hardy compels us to like him, to feel grief for his fall; we are like the old lady who cried out during a performance of *Othello* 'Oh why can't the great black fool SEE!'

If we look at him objectively there is plenty to dislike in Henchard. He is violent, cruel, jealous, domineering: he can lie to one man and browbeat another. But we are made to realise that each of these actions arises out of the excess of some good quality and so we realise, as Hardy intended, that the dull uniform grey of Farfrae (the decent but cold-gutted Scot, who is so subtly contrasted with Henchard throughout) is not necessarily preferable to the violent black and white of Henchard. Farfrae's ambition, snobbishness and occasional meanness are all touched in, acidly enough to make us ask, 'What is goodness?', and perhaps Elizabeth Jane provides the answer. She is a 'point of rest' between the two men, with plenty of sense and a marked distrust of 'externals'. These three and their close relations provide an example of the pattern Hardy liked to work to—a small close-knit group of characters, examined in depth; and though I shall necessarily dwell on Henchard a good deal, for all his dominant role it is upon the fine balance maintained between these three that Hardy's success in this book depends.

It is not predominantly a love story: rather it is a complex network of human relationships enclosed in a fairly narrow frame where, for once, Nature plays a significantly smaller part than human nature. It is therefore the best place to study Hardy's treatment of character. How does he set about this task? First of all and typically, we are given a physical description of Henchard, including hints that his movements betray his character, e.g., 'In the turn and plant of each foot there was a dogged and cynical indifference'. He nods 'with some superciliousness'. Gradually and subtly the portrait is darkened. Henchard's own speeches betray him as frustrated and ambitious. He evinces no love for his wife or daughter, drinks away his money, becomes 'fuddled', then obstinate, and at length sells his wife for five guineas. 'Ah what a cruelty is the poor soul married to', says one onlooker. But Hardy, though he doesn't spare Henchard, contrives a situation which forces upon him a choice he would probably rather avoid. 'Up to this moment', we are told, it is doubtful if he 'was in earnest'. Now his wife, who has very little sense, produces the very remark that is bound to provoke a crisis. 'Mind', she says, 'it's a joke no longer'. It isn't the money that Henchard takes up, so much as his wife's challenge to his imperious temper, exacerbated by drink, the silent contempt of the onlookers and stored resentment at his own lack of success which he has, in part, attributed to her. This is not a cold, calculating decision, but one taken in the heat of the moment. It isn't in Henchard's character to give an inch when forced into a corner, as he is here, and much as we feel for his wife and child, we also feel some sympathy for him as he stands, 'a stolid look of concern' on his face, after his wife has flung her wedding-ring at him.

I have dwelt on this scene because it provides the pattern for many others. Hardy heaps up significant descriptive phrases like 'rough and ready perceptions', 'sledge-hammer directness'. Yet Henchard is, he admits, a 'rule of thumb man': 'strength and bustle have built up his business', for 'he was mentally and physically unfit for grubbing subtleties from soiled paper'. Now 'judgment and knowledge are what (will) keep it established'. Henchard turns to Farfrae for these qualities, and Farfrae undoubtedly possesses them. But it is these very qualities which, ironically, precipitate the first clash between Farfrae and his employer (when Henchard has forced Abel Whittle to work in his shirt as a punishment for lateness). The scene closely parallels the 'wife auction', for Farfrae actually remarks, 'This JOKE has been carried far enough'. Surely this is deliberate patterning by Hardy. The man who has destroyed his wife's loyalty now destroys Farfrae's, and in the end—worst of all— he shatters the fine flower of all the rest, Elizabeth Jane's trust in him. Henchard then is consistent, but consistency isn't enough in a character, and some of Hardy's most consistent people are his least convincing.

Hardy worked best when he was drawing characters with some very strongly marked quality of mind. What, then, is the dominant note in Henchard? Hardy hits upon a means of making Henchard as much the victim as the agent of the misfortunes that fall on him, by endowing him with a quality I can only call 'spiritual hamfistedness'. He is incapable of being lukewarm. His bullying of Abel Whittle, the coal he sends to Abel's old mother—these are two sides of the same coin; not, as they seem, inconsistencies. Until nearly the end of the book Henchard blunders about like a bull in the china shop of human susceptibilities. He is 'unruly volcanic stuff', 'a headstrong stunpoll'; his 'diplomacy is like a buffalo's'; he is only able to express his true self in action, where Hardy shows us the real nobility of the man. When it matters he will sacrifice anything, even his own pride, to justice, so long as he can see what is just. Here we can see the perfect balance Hardy maintains at his best, for we should be quite wrong to judge Henchard solely by what he says. Words to him are two-edged weapons; they often betray him. Thus he speaks 'with withering humility' to Lucetta when he is a labourer and she is Farfrae's wife: 'Ah ma'am, we of the lower classes know nothing of the gay leisure that such as you enjoy.' Yet when she sends him a letter that would destroy Farfrae's love for ever if he saw it—' "Poor fool" said Henchard with fond savagery, and he threw the letter in the fire'. He sells his gold watch to help one of his poorest creditors after his bankruptcy, and when the Furmity woman reveals his shameful past in the court where Henchard is magistrate and the Clerk intends to silence her—' "No. 'Tis true." The words came from Henchard. " 'Tis true as light", he said slowly. "And to keep out of any temptation to treat her hard for her revenge, I'll leave her to you." ' There is nothing more noble in any of the Wessex novels than this, and Henchard's desperate, unrelenting and futile efforts to bring Farfrae back to his dying wife are on a par with it. Hardy's triumph here is to take a character whose nature is basically simple, and show how complex a web of tragedy he may weave for himself out of what is not so much a flaw in his character as an excess, and how out of unbalanced 'large-heartedness' a 'dark ruin' can be built.

There is something terrible about the way Henchard, when he feels that though a 'reprobate . . . even I be in Somebody's hand', is thrown down again. At last he wins through to that 'wisdom' he so much needs! But this is after he has judged himself too harshly and left Elizabeth Jane with these heart-rending words: '. . . Don't let my sins . . . cause 'ee quite to forget that though I loved 'ee late, I loved 'ee well.' This is not the Henchard who was described as 'a Prince of Darkness', and the 'wisdom has come pari passu [i.e., at the same time as] with the departure of the zest for doing'. Henchard ceases to 'value himself' and cannot, in the end, even bother to explain to Elizabeth Jane why he lied to Newson. He leaves behind the caged singing-bird, pathetic symbol of his child-like trust that all may yet be well, and goes off to die. I don't think he died 'like a maddened bull, defiant to the last', myself. His tragedy is seen best in two small phrases: on the first page we hear of his 'measured springless walk'; on the last Whittle 'zeed that he wambled and could hardly drag along'. He has come to the end of the road. Seen in this light, Henchard's will isn't so much an act of defiance as one of acceptance. Henchard places no value on himself and expects no one else to do so either. Humility, once so lacking, is now absolute, and Elizabeth Jane reads bitterness into Henchard's last words because she blames herself. Henchard's main wish is to spare her grief—something he feels he has always failed to do, and this is in keeping with Hardy's conception of him.

Of the other characters, less need be said. None of them, however, is a failure; each is drawn in just sufficient depth for the purpose Hardy has in mind, and in each case an appropriate technique is used. Elizabeth Jane is perhaps as near as anyone to Hardy's ideal woman. By contrasting her with the wayward, imprudent Lucetta, 'a mere shadow of her menfolk', he stresses Elizabeth's quiet charm. Yet she has feelings, though they aren't on the surface, and where Hardy painted in Henchard with great sweeping strokes (like some vast portrait in oils), Elizabeth Jane is delicately etched with a multitude of small touches. Her desire, even as a child, is 'to see, hear and understand', and she has what no one else around her has—balance, or as Hardy puts it in a telling phrase, 'the crystalline sphere of a straightforward mind'. But she isn't remote; she is 'willing to sacrifice her personal comfort and dignity to the common weal', and she has depth of feeling. Her 'innate perceptiveness'—again a quality the others all lack—stands out and is shown when she says, looking at her useless 'finery', 'Better sell all this and buy books'. Her final comment, 'But there's no altering—so it must be', is Hardy speaking, and he succeeds in the uncommonly difficult task of making the small, steady flame of her gentle spirit visible against those crackling bonfires of emotion, Henchard and Lucetta.

What has been said of *The Mayor of Casterbridge* cannot,

unfortunately, be said of all Hardy's books. Often his characters are by no means as fully or as craftily drawn, but the strong bold lines of Henchard's character here provide the clue to Hardy's success elsewhere. Whenever he can focus on one or two individuals the full blaze of his creative imagination, they come to life at once.

'THE WOODLANDERS', AND HARDY'S STYLE AND METHOD

The Woodlanders attracted a more unanimous chorus of critical praise when it first appeared in 1886 than any of Hardy's previous novels. Hardy himself thought it one of his best—'I think I like it as a story best of all', he wrote. Unquestionably it contains much of Hardy's finest writing; the many descriptions of the woods at different seasons and at all hours of the day and night, for example, are among his finest. On the other hand there are plenty of examples of Hardy's style at its least attractive, and his method of construction—here, as usual, basically strong and simple—also reveals flaws of the kind that mar and weaken several other novels.

First the construction, which is straightforward enough. Hardy took as his setting the 'Hintocks' . . . 'one of these sequestered spots outside the gates of the world where dramas of a grandeur and unity truly Sophoclean are enacted in the real by virtue of the concentrated passions and closely knit interdependence of the lives therein'. Here in fact Hardy reveals his method in all his most successful books. If we add to this formula that the chief characters are few and closely linked by powerful emotional ties, we have the essential framework of nearly all the Wessex novels.

In *The Woodlanders*, Dr. Fitzpiers attracts and is attracted by three strongly contrasted women, Felice Charmond, Suke Damson, and Grace Melbury, who, so far as he is concerned, represent three different aspects of love. Felice stands for the wild, irrational, neck-or-nothing kind, Suke for plain physical lust, and Grace for a mixture of calculation, fascination and idealisation. Hardy's method is to spin these four around in a hectic emotional roundabout, while the noble and constant

Giles Winterborne, who loves Grace single-mindedly, and Marty South who loves him, stand looking on, both ultimately suffering tragedy from being dragged into the whirl of passion as participants. The novel is in fact about constancy and inconstancy in love. This is a tightly-woven theme, and so long as it is worked out within the confines and against the daily life of Mellstock itself, it remains wholly convincing. Among many other examples of Hardy's skill when at home in Wessex, so to speak, are the sad humour with which he conveys how Giles's party to welcome Grace offends her 'educated' taste, and the mixture of pathos and sardonic insight which he displays in telling of the old Midsummer Eve rites, where Fitzpiers first ousts Giles by catching Grace as she runs along the path, and straightaway afterwards seduces Suke Damson in a hayfield, so getting both the gilt and the gingerbread. Both these incidents are perfectly done and totally believable. So is Grace's cry to Giles, who has chivalrously given up his hut to her and now lies dying out in the storm: 'Come to me! I don't mind what they say or what they think any more'.

On the other hand, this novel demonstrates to perfection exactly what happens when Hardy strays outside his own territory. The pistol-packing 'passionate gentleman from South Carolina', who pursues and in the end (most conveniently) shoots Felice, is merely laughable. All the same, similar examples of barefaced 'anything goes' contrivance arouse our irritation all too frequently in Hardy's books. A far more serious fault is the way in which, the moment we enter Hintock House with Fitzpiers and Mrs. Charmond, an absurdly 'elevated' manner of narration and a ludicrously affected 'High Society' style of speech descend like a fog upon the book. The whole of Chapter 36 exemplifies what is, beyond question, Hardy's Achilles heel as a novelist. As Felice cries out '. . . if heaven would only give (me) strength—but heaven never did', we can't help visualising her clutching her brow in the best melodramatic style. It is hard to keep a straight face when the bloody apparition of Fitzpiers's head at the window is followed by this prize example of Hardy's 'fine writing': '. . . it met her frightened eyes like a replica of the Sudarium of Saint Veronica'. This is hardly the moment for a short course in art criticism, one feels. Hardy's vocabulary is also execrable at this point: phrases like 'aforesaid nooks' and 'possible concatenation of events' jar everywhere on our ears, and for the 'half-dead' Fitzpiers to quote from Shakespeare and the Bible while gasping out his misfortunes to Felice adds the finishing touch of absurdity. (He's crawled more than a mile on his hands and knees already.)

About Hardy's method then, it may be said that, while fundamentally sound, it is always liable to go to pieces when Hardy departs from a severely restricted range of character and incident. The passages just quoted, however, show grave faults of style as well as of construction, and in fact Hardy has no such thing as an everyday style such as most authors can command. We simply have to accept a perpetual oscillation between 'Splendours and Miseries'—an oscillation perhaps more marked in *The Woodlanders* than elsewhere. There are miracles of expression:

> 'Now, my own, own love', she whispered, 'you are mine, and on'y mine; for she has forgot 'ee at last, although for her you died! But I—whenever I lie down I'll think of 'ee. Whenever I plant the young larches I'll think that none can plant as you planted; and whenever I split a gad, and whenever I turn the cider wring, I'll say none could do it like you. If ever I forget your name let me forget home and heaven! . . . But no, no, my love, I never can forget 'ee; for you was a good man, and did good things!'

This is Marty's lament for Giles. Here Hardy is not so much using rustic speech—dialect is barely hinted at—as employing a simple, somewhat repetitive and strongly rhythmic *style* to achieve an effect which moves us deeply because it seems quite uncontrived. Marty South's nature is mirrored in her speech; her imagery is drawn from the woods which she knew as well as Giles. But perhaps most important of all, there are, as Hardy knew, certain words which it is impossible to wear out by over-use. These are largely words of Anglo-Saxon origin, and it is notable that hardly a word in Marty's speech is of Latin derivation. Her speech indeed is an example of Hardy's most uniformly successful style—a style which we might call 'Wessex Conversational'. It is flexible. It can rise to heights of feeling as we have just seen, or it can be used for perfectly ordinary purposes, like Creedle's remarks on the slug which had strayed on to Grace's plate:

> 'God forbid that a *live* slug should be seed on any plate of vittles that's served by Robert Creedle. . . . But Lord, there; I don't mind 'em myself—them green ones; for they were born on cabbage and they've lived on cabbage, so they must be made of cabbage.'

XII

This style almost never lets Hardy down. Regrettably he had, as he saw it, another duty to perform, namely to write in a style which I shall call 'Society Conversational'. When one of Hardy's society characters opens his mouth, even the most devoted reader is often tempted to shut his book. At moments of high emotion Felice *can* speak like a human being. But more often than not she utters phrases like this: 'Some monstrous calumnies are afloat!'; and Grace isn't much better with her reflection: 'Can it be that cruel propriety is killing the dearest heart that ever woman clasped to her own!' Long latinate words are generally the culprits, as they are here. They are also a feature of another of Hardy's styles, which might be termed the 'Self-conscious Literary', of which 'It had soothed her perturbed spirit better than all the opiates in the pharmacopoeia' is an average example, consisting of a quotation from *Hamlet* and two jaw-cracking latinisms. The marks of the style are a heavy top-dressing of quotation and reference to the arts; scraps of Latin, French and German; odds and ends of Scandinavian myth, and goodness knows what else. It is not so much the presence of these oddly assorted scraps of general knowledge and dictionary-scrapings that is tedious, but the way Hardy throws them in by the fistful as if they were candied peel and the novel a Christmas pudding. Here he *was* naïve—distrusting his own good sense of what was fitting for what was, he supposed, 'correct'.

Hardy's worst style is 'Reach-me-down Journalese', but luckily it is rare. It is exemplified in 'Having concluded her examination of this now uselessly commodious edifice . . .'.

Yet again there is 'Straightforward Narrative', where Hardy hasn't anything particular in mind but getting on with the story. This doesn't need illustrating, but Hardy's 'Landscape' style—which is one of the glories of *The Woodlanders* and which is used in innumerable passages to picture the woods at all seasons—constitutes his greatest achievement in prose. One sentence will do to exemplify it:

> They went noiselessly over mats of starry moss, rustled through interspersed tracts of leaves, skirted trunks with spreading roots whose mossed rinds made them like hands wearing green gloves; elbowed old elms and ashes with great forks, in which stood pools of water that overflowed on rainy days and ran down their stems in green cascades.

VIII

Exactness, lucidity, the kind of intensity and accuracy that only comes from intimate and loving acquaintance with the thing described, the kind of meditation that arises naturally from the things considered—these are the hallmarks of this style. A single sentence describing the apple country: 'Over the vale the air was blue as sapphire—such a blue as outside that apple valley was never seen', perhaps also symbolises the beauty, richness and peace that none of the characters will ever attain. For Hardy's finest descriptions do more than simply describe, they add a whole dimension of feeling to his work.

Hardy then has not one but many styles, and it is useless to deny that some are regrettable. If what you want is an even, unruffled flow of lucid, unemphatic prose, you will have to look elsewhere. For my part, I am prepared to put up with the bad parts for the sake of the good, just as I am ready to be jolted about on a mountain road in order to enjoy the view from the summit.

'JUDE THE OBSCURE' AND HARDY'S THOUGHT

I said earlier that good novels make us think. *Jude* certainly does this, and the question is, What does Hardy want us to think about? What issues is he raising? In *Jude*, of course, the author clearly has a philosophical axe to grind, and Hardy thought his work was disliked because, he said, 'Britons hate ideas'. What they really disliked was Hardy's forthright treatment of problems arising out of marriage and divorce. More particularly, the highly sensitive nostrils of Mrs. Grundy detected the unmentionable odour of sex. The scene where Arabella throws an (obviously symbolic) pig's pizzle at Jude, and the subsequent seduction—whether of Arabella or Jude it is hard to say—set them off in full cry; 'a novel of lubricity' ... 'filth and defilement' ... 'coarseness beyond belief' are samples of what passed for criticism in a period when the book-borrowing public demanded the rigid observation in fiction of conventions already crumbling away in fact.

At this distance we can see how irrelevant it all was. *Jude* now appears to be what Hardy always called it, 'a moral book', grimly, even frighteningly insistent on its major theme, the inevitable clash between 'the ideal life a man wished to lead and the squalid real life he was forced to lead', as Hardy put it in a letter to his friend Gosse. The word 'theme' had perhaps better be defined. It means, roughly, the underlying aims of the novelist in so far as they aren't embodied in the story. For example, 'The serpent tempted Eve to eat an apple' is a *story*. The *theme* is obedience to God's will. Few novels are without some sort of theme (even the James Bond series stress the desirability of 'keeping the upper lip STIFF', as Gerard Hoffnung used to say), and Hardy nearly always has at least one, and often two or three, in hand. When we talk of Hardy's 'thought', then, we mean both ideas expressed point blank (for instance, 'Love has its own dark morality when rivalry enters in') and ideas conveyed more or less indirectly as part of the novel's theme or themes, of which the sharp contrast between the new Hymn which so much impresses Jude, and its greedy, vain composer, who is deserting music to sell wine, is a good, concise example of the contrast between illusion and reality which continually recurs in various forms. This contrast, which is also expressed in terms of what Hardy called 'the deadly war between flesh and spirit', is more consistently and fully developed in *Jude* than in any of Hardy's other books. *Jude*, however, is also 'about' a number of other things; too many, perhaps. Hardy is deeply concerned about the difficulties of the poor student's ever getting any higher education at all. Jude's failure to get into Christminster is, it is true, only part of a larger pattern. 'Predestinate Jude's' story is that of successive failures. Even so he was 'elbowed off the pavement by the millionaire's sons', says Sue. Still, the difference between Jude's first coming to Oxford, his gloomy vision (as he wanders in twilit streets) of the mighty dead speaking to him one by one, and his last disillusioned departure (besides making a deeper impression than Hardy's bitter direct criticisms) fits into the general theme very well. But—and this is important —Hardy is also concerned with improving the status of women in society, demanding reform of the divorce laws, criticising the zealous excesses of Anglo-Catholicism, hitting out at provincial prudishness, exposing the weakness of the educational system with especial reference to teacher training, drawing attention to the narrow-mindedness of church-going people, and even with an attack on the gin-trap. It's fair to say that *Jude* carries altogether too heavy a load of good intentions; at times the framework of the novel creaks and groans a bit with the stresses Hardy puts on it in order to get everything in.

Despite this, *Jude* remains an impressive novel, which may even today shock us by its ruthlessness, of which the hanging of children, 'done because we were too menny', is the best-known example, but which isn't in fact simply an expression of Hardy's utter gloom and pessimism, as a superficial reader is likely to suppose. Hardy isn't just saying: ' 'Ere we suffer grief and pain: Over the road it's just the same'. The book is, as he points out, a 'tragedy of unfulfilled aims' and since, to borrow Thackeray's phrase, 'What man has his desire, or having it is satisfied?', it is to some extent universal. On the other hand, Jude is an 'outsider'; both he and Sue are 'too thin-skinned, horribly sensitive', and Sue is 'a sort of Fay or Sprite . . . not a woman', and has 'a curious double nature'. Both, too, have a dangerous heredity, which may well make for 'two bitters in one dish'. Hardy is determined to show us that Sue and Jude are odd fish, that their predicament is not representative but grows out of their particular temperaments and personalities. Further to stress this he gives us in Phillotson and Arabella two people, both conventional in their own way, and, as a point of normality, the widow Edlin whose attitude is typified by: 'Nobody thought o' being afeard o' matrimony in my time, nor of much else but a cannon-ball or empty cupboard! Why, when I and my poor man were married we thought no more o't than a game o' dibs!' Hardy doesn't suggest that the world is always cruel to everyone—only to those with a 'morbid' conviction of their own difference, and certainly we aren't meant to approve wholeheartedly of Sue and Jude either, though we pity them. For Jude is cruel to Sue, and Sue to Jude, on several occasions.

What then is the real theme of the book if it is not simply to present the world, in Dr. Johnson's phrase, as 'bursting with sin and misery'? Hardy said that it contained 'a good deal that (is) universal', and he refers to 'the fret and fever, derision and dis- aster that . . . press in the wake of the strongest passion known to humanity'. It is towards love that Hardy directs the main current of his thought in *Jude*. He sees it for what it is, a force in human affairs that is subtle, profound, wide-ranging and often tragic in its consequences. He views it with an eye shrewd and compassionate but above all utterly honest.

First Hardy presents us with Jude's early, pure, idealistic love for Christminster, 'the heavenly Jerusalem' . . . 'the city of light'. Jude's passion stands here for that totally unselfish, disinterested love which most of us are at some time capable of, though the objects of it may vary. Even this ideal suffers a jolt when Jude learns that there is no 'law of transmutation'; that Latin and Greek mean '. . . years of plodding'. So for the first, but by no means the last time, Reality destroys Illusion, and this is a con- stantly recurring theme.

Next Jude meets Arabella and falls in love with her. Though his love is only 'physical', it doesn't lack intensity. When Arabella was absent ' . . . a void was in [Jude] which nothing could fill'. There is nothing wrong with this in itself, but Hardy sharply points out the flaw in it. Jude has fooled himself. He realises that Arabella 'isn't worth much', but 'his *idea* of her was the thing of most consequence'. Jude isn't blind; he knows he is wrong; and Hardy here stresses the crucial importance of absolute honesty in love. This too is a central theme of *Jude*.

It is further demonstrated in Phillotson, who suffers a terrible awakening from his 'dream of great beauty'. But this is partly Phillotson's fault. Hardy is at pains to show that Phillotson deceives himself, seeing Sue as he wants to see her, not as she is. Similarly, Sue isn't really honest with herself either. Over the question of her marriage to Phillotson she ignored the true promptings of her heart, as she admits when challenged by the dying Aunt Drusilla. Each of the three, then, who form the central triangle of the book, has betrayed what Keats called 'the holiness of the heart's affections'.

The second 'movement' of the novel begins at this point, with the heart-rending scene where Jude kills a trapped and tormented rabbit to put it out of its misery, and so plunges unwittingly into his own. He speaks to Sue at her window. He abandons his principles: 'My doctrines and I begin to part company', he says; 'let them go. Let me help you even if I do love you . . .'. Sue kisses him, a 'scarcely perceptible kiss on the top of his head'. From such a small beginning, Hardy suggests, disaster may spring, and from now on Jude and Sue try to pursue a life in which they give up 'all for love'. Jude burns his books, a significant little scene; Sue leaves Phillotson, who appears at this point the noblest of the three. The two begin their foredoomed attempt to live out an ideal—an ideal which Phillotson shrewdly describes as 'Shelleyan'. Like Shelley, whom Hardy admired (though he saw through his platonic ideas), they 'fall upon the thorns of life'. Their ideal is never attained, that is the tragedy. It was, Hardy tells us, unattainable. But, and this is most important, Hardy does not condemn them for trying to attain it, nor does he suggest that it is altogether an illusion. He simply shows that Sue and Jude are not in reality the ideally matched couple they suppose themselves to be. They still deceive themselves and one another. Sue's love for Jude isn't physical at all (just as Arabella's was nothing else): so, as Hardy said in a letter to Edmund Gosse, Jude has 'never possessed her as fully as he desires'. In consequence, Jude wavers, desiring from Sue what only Arabella could have given him. Sue asks from Jude something that no man could give her, something which, as Hardy indicates, no woman has a right to expect—a combination of the most intense spiritual adoration with an entire absence of physical fulfilment. Hardy discusses their predicament with sad wisdom. They think they can defy society, they cannot; they think they can defy Nature (or at least Sue does) but they cannot; and perhaps Hardy implies that love as totally self-centred as theirs where the world is locked out altogether, must be self-destructive. Perhaps—but one cannot be sure. For there is the incident of the Flower Show:

> Sue's usually pale cheeks reflected the pink of the tinted roses at which she gazed, for . . . the excitement of a day's outing with Jude had quickened her blood and made her eyes sparkle with vivacity. . . . She adored roses . . . and put her face within an inch of their blooms to smell them. 'I should like to push my face into them, the dears', she said. 'But I suppose it is against the rules to touch them—isn't it, Jude?'. 'Yes, you baby', said he; and then playfully gave her a little push, so that her nose went among the petals.
>
> 5, V

Somehow Hardy has gathered all their odd, unworldly, fragile, yet strangely moving happiness up into that. No great novelist imposes his thought upon us. When we put down this book our first feeling may well be one of resentment at the unfairness of Jude's fate, at his death, far from Sue and in despair, with Job's terrible words on his lips: 'Let the day perish wherein I was born'. But the deep continuous probing Hardy has carried out will have its effect if we let it sink in. We are made to realise that, as Hardy puts it, 'the essence of love is its gratuitousness' (i.e., it is freely given and cannot be bought or sold). Maybe Jude's visions are all false; yet, in a way, it is the radiancy of these visions and Jude's devotion to them which matter. With his usual unerring sense of a fitting conclusion, Hardy leaves the last word with Arabella. She has been told that Sue has 'found peace'. Arabella says, 'She may swear that on her knees to the holy cross upon her necklace till she's hoarse, but it won't be true! She's never found peace since she left his arms, and never will again till she's as he is now!'

Introduction. When Hardy wrote this novel as a serial for the *Cornhill Magazine*, he was living in his old home at Bockhampton. He tells us that some of the book was actually written on '. . . white chips left by the woodcutters, or pieces of stone or slate', and that while he was working on the book, he also talked to members of the 'Mellstock' choir, and for the last time '. . . assisted at his father's cider-making'. All of this, no doubt, helps to account for the special flavour of this tale, which, more than any other, seems to have the authentic touch and taste and smell of the countryside in it; for, as Hardy wrote to Leslie Stephen, he found it 'a great advantage to be actually among the people the book described, at the time of describing them'. The story is set in and around 'Weatherbury', which was almost on Hardy's doorstep. Indeed, he even mentions 'Weatherbury Eweleaze', scene of one of his poems to Tryphena Sparks, while all that part of Wessex was uncommonly well known to him, and thick with memories and associations.

As a result, *Far From the Madding Crowd* has a solidity of setting and character which could only come from profound knowledge and an integrity of treatment based on truth to life as it is, or rather was, in such small hamlets, for Hardy laments, in his Preface, the 'break of continuity in local history'. The book richly deserved its initial success, which made Hardy quite a prosperous and sought-after writer. It is the first of his major novels, and to my mind one of the very finest. In considering it, and *Tess of the D'Urbervilles*, which follows, I shall continue to make use of the categories I employed in discussing previous novels, beginning with:

Construction and Plot. Hardy's basic plot is very simple. Gabriel Oak, a small farmer (his name is significant, for we are told on page three that he 'wears well'), sees Bathsheba Everdene, whom

Hardy depicts—with one of those flashes of visual imagination which light up his best work—sitting on a farm cart, practising her smile in a mirror. Though flirtatious and immature, she is beautiful and fascinating. Oak falls in love with her and soon proposes, in rather a bull-at-a-gate manner. She refuses him, though not all that definitely. Hardy then contrives a tremendous reversal of fortune for both. Oak loses all he has in a disastrous sheep stampede while Bathsheba becomes, by inheritance, a very wealthy tenant farmer, and later Oak's employer. After being drawn so close together, they are now hurled apart, apparently for ever; the sort of violent upheaval Hardy often makes use of in his novels, to promote contrast.

After a quiet opening, the long central section of the book begins. This consists of the wild vicissitudes which Bathsheba experiences in love and marriage. These involve first the apparently dull but in fact highly inflammable Farmer Boldwood, whom Bathsheba 'idly' beguiles by means of a Valentine; then the superficially attractive but cruel and amoral Sergeant Troy, whom she marries in haste, to repent at leisure. She is drawn to Boldwood again after Troy's apparent death, and a tragic climax follows, involving both. But after all the tumult and suffering, Oak is still there, the 'faithful man', with a love that now includes understanding and sympathy, to claim Bathsheba, who has gone through the fire to become a wiser woman, able now to rate Oak at his true worth, so that the novel closes as quietly as it began.

This is a firm outline, but Hardy's skill in construction is chiefly apparent in his subtle use of contrast throughout the book. The plot is developed by means of a series of encounters between the main characters. These 'confrontations' map out their changing relationships and are occasionally varied by direct comments from Hardy (for example, his character-sketches of Boldwood and Troy, each of which fills a chapter). There is plenty of pace and surprise in *Far From the Madding Crowd*, swiftly moving action like the pursuit of the supposed horse-thieves alternating with the slow timeless conversation at Warren's malthouse. Nevertheless, all the characters are swept along; some, like Bathsheba and Troy, darting about like quick-silver, some, like poor Fanny Robin, drifting with the current, some like Oak, sturdily swimming against the tide, in the great river of Time represented here by the procession of the seasons. For it is the essence of Hardy's achievement in this book to have interspersed with his human drama scenes drawn from the unending cycle of the farmer's year. Lambing, shearing, sheep-dipping, hay-making—all go on indifferent to the erratic antics of the human actors, and it is this continual contrast which gives the book much of its power. Hardy has succeeded in so completely intertwining man and his environment as to oblige his readers to realise the entire dependence of one on the other. Indeed it is as if the Land itself were a character, speaking to us at times through men like Coggan, when he replies to Oak, who has rebuked him for stopping to drink when bringing Fanny Robin's body home:

> 'If she'd been alive, I would have been the first to help her. If she now wanted vittles and drink, I'd pay for it, money down. But she's dead, and no speed of ours would bring her to life. . . . Drink, shepherd, and be friends, for tomorrow we may be like her.'
>
> 42

Coincidences do occur in *Far From the Madding Crowd*, but they aren't overdone. Indeed most of the flaws that mar Hardy's other novels are entirely absent. This is because, in effect, he is at home, on his own ground. Throughout the book he remains there, writing always of what he knew best. As a consequence this is his best constructed, most believable novel.

Thought. This isn't a novel of ideas like *Jude the Obscure*, and Hardy seldom gives us extended reflections on life in it. Nevertheless, it does contain important elements of Hardy's thought, though these are generally evolved out of the action of the book rather than flatly stated, which is on the whole a distinct advantage. It is often said that Hardy's attitude in this book is 'fatalistic'—that, to quote Webster, 'We are only the stars' tennis-balls, struck and banded/Which way please them'. Certainly Hardy commends Oak's 'indifference to fate', but

Troy is likewise pretty indifferent to fate, and he is hardly commendable. Obviously the *reasons* for these attitudes are more important than the attitudes themselves. The episode where a stray dog which has supported the dying Fanny Robin during her last journey to the Casterbridge Union is 'stoned away' is also supposed to be evidence of Hardy's gloomy view of human existence. But we must be careful of attaching too much importance to isolated incidents and comments, or for that matter to the tags with which Hardy attempted to give a neat finish to the serial chapters. Similarly, we can't lay Troy's clever cynicisms about women at Hardy's door: he intended Troy to appear a clever man with his eye on the main chance, and though there is some truth in what he says, there is much more opportunism. In fact there are a good many side-hits (at marriage as a 'respectable folly', for instance), but the main line of Hardy's thought is clear enough, and its development can be traced through the book. For what he is really considering is the same problem as he later treated more extensively in *Jude the Obscure*. The question Hardy asks is, 'What is the nature of love?' He gives his answer at the end of the book:

> 'Substantial affection . . . the only love which is as strong as death . . . arises when two who are thrown together begin first by knowing the rougher sides of each other's character, and the best not till further on.'

57

The whole book has been working up to this, for all the various kinds of love have been flawed, and Hardy is at pains in each case to indicate the flaw. Thus, though Oak's first proposal to Bathsheba is more comic than serious, it's made clear that Oak is infatuated and doesn't see her as she really is. Nevertheless, Oak is the only one of the major characters who doesn't put on an act but is utterly himself from start to finish. Even Boldwood, cruelly as he suffers, is to some extent the agent of his own misfortune. He refuses even to admit that Bathsheba *might* be merely frivolous. Similarly, Bathsheba is self-deceived. As her behaviour to all three suitors shows, she lives in a world of romantic fantasy.

Hardy talks of Boldwood's 'blindness' and Bathsheba's 'insensibility': she can reason well, he tells us, 'where her heart is not involved'. This is of course what delivers her into Troy's hands. She refuses to admit that he is a 'flatterer', though she knows that he is insincere, and has even said so. She even tries to make Liddy, her honest little servant-girl, 'Solemnly swear . . . that it is all lies they say about him, that he *cannot* be bad'.

Liddy won't agree, and Bathsheba doesn't really convince herself. But like Boldwood, and Troy for that matter, she prefers her ideal notion of love to the truth which stares her in the face. In the same way Troy thinks he can have his cake and eat it too. In the end all these self-deluding characters discover the truth at desperate cost. In *Far From the Madding Crowd*, full as it is of pity for the victims of this delusion, Hardy is concerned above all to show that love cannot be treated lightly, and to convey the immense importance of constancy. In the end it is the love 'that seeketh not her own' which matters. Only when Oak and Bathsheba have fully realised this can they marry with some assurance of happiness.

Style. In this book Hardy is as assured a writer as he ever became: his stylistic lapses are indeed fewer than in most of the later novels. As I have said, Hardy's style is always very much dependent on his subject. The absence of society characters means that the 'Society Conversational' style is absent too. The setting in rural Dorset also precludes much use of the 'Self-conscious Literary' style, and Hardy's deep involvement with this story stops him resorting to 'Reach-me-down Journalese'. As a result you can open a page at random and find phrases, sentences and whole paragraphs as good as Hardy ever wrote. By way of proving this I opened the book on:

'Too much liquor is bad and leads us to the horned man in the smoky house.'

This is closely followed by Mark Clark's comment on Churchmen (as opposed to Nonconformists):

'We . . . must have it all printed aforehand, or, dang it all, we should no more know what to say to a great gaffer like the Lord than babes unborn.'

42

There is a very great deal of this vintage 'Wessex Conversation' in *Far From the Madding Crowd*, and the temptation to quote at length is hard to resist. There is only room for one more example here, the splendid dialogue between Coggan and Jacob:

> 'But for a drink of really noble class that brought you no nearer to the dark man than you were afore you begun, there was none like those in Farmer Everdene's kitchen. Not a single damn allowed; no, not a bare poor one, even at the most cheerful moment when all were blindest, though the good old word of sin thrown in here and there at such times is a great relief to a merry soul.'
>
> 'True', said the maltster. 'Nater requires her swearing at the regular times or she's not herself; and unholy exclamations is a necessity of life.'

8

The easy flow of this, the detail, the dry humour, are all set down by Hardy with a relish which we share. But Hardy isn't just a recorder. Only he would have thought of something at once as true and as funny as the maltster's last remark, only he would have written 'good old word of sin'.

Hardy's style is every bit as masterly in descriptive passages— both those relating to people, like the snapshot of Oak's face 'rising like the moon behind the hedge', and incidents like those entitled 'The Fire' and 'The Storm'. Both are notable examples of his skill in creating a sense of pace and urgency. His use of significant detail adds snap and vigour to scenes of action. He isn't impeccable, of course. To call Bathsheba's home a 'mouldy pile' is to use a well-worn cliché. But these lapses are few and hardly merit notice.

Hardy's 'Landscape' style is particularly well shown in this book: the description of a sunset, already quoted on page 111 is an especially fine example. But there are many others almost equally good—this description of heat, for instance:

> 'The Oat-harvest began, and all the men were afield under a mono-chromatic Lammas sky, amid the trembling air and short shadows of

noon. Indoors nothing was to be heard save the droning of blue-bottle flies; out of doors the whetting of scythes and the hiss of tressy oatears rubbing together as their perpendicular stalks of amber-yellow fell heavily to each swath.'

33

Nothing could be more concrete and more precise than that. The heat is almost felt, and the sounds are wonderfully conveyed by words like 'droning', 'whetting', 'scythes', 'hiss' and 'tressy oatears'. Besides this almost cinematic accuracy, Hardy can produce passages of great beauty which are more poetic in quality. He can do this in a single sentence, e.g.:

'The confused beginnings of many birds' songs spread into the healthy air; and the wan blue of the heaven was here and there coated with thin webs of incorporeal cloud which were of no effect in obscuring day.'

34

This is very close to blank verse: indeed three lines are quite regular.

I shall conclude with an example of Hardy at his most opulent and glowing:

Bathsheba's singing was soft and rather tremulous at first, but it soon swelled to a steady clearness. . . .

For his bride a soldier sought her,
And a winning tongue had he:
On the banks of Allan Water
None was gay as she!

In addition to the dulcet piping of Gabriel's flute, Boldwood supplied a bass in his customary profound voice, uttering his notes so softly, however, as to abstain entirely from making anything like an ordinary duet of the song; they rather formed a rich un-explored shadow, which threw their tones into relief. The shearers reclined against each other as at suppers in the early ages of the world, and so silent and absorbed were they that her breathing could almost be heard between the bars; and at the end of the ballad, when the last tone loitered on to an inexpressible close, there arose that buzz of pleasure which is the attar of applause.

23

Here the loving detail of the scene is combined with images of music, beauty, peace, and pastoral life, which blend to make a magical impression that ultimately defies analysis. This is the still centre of the book, where the two nobler rivals and Bathsheba are joined for a moment in a harmony which is perhaps significant of their real unity (all three 'belong' to the land) as it is certainly poignantly fragile. Hardy subtly suggests the stillness, together with the feeling of richness and fulfilment, by his style, employing suggestive phrases and adjectives to great effect. Consider the sequence: 'dulcet piping . . . flute . . . bass . . . profound . . . softly . . . shadow'. It produces an effect of increasing silence and concentration, to which the 'buzz of pleasure' is the perfect counter. The whole scene is idyllic, as the reference to the 'early ages of the world' makes clear, yet in no way sentimentalised or unreal. We feel this happened exactly as it is told, yet also somehow that we have strayed into another country 'Where neither sorrow comes, nor tired old age'; and this delicate balance between truth of fact and truth of emotion is the mark of Hardy's style throughout the book. Nowhere else in the Wessex novels is he more at ease, more totally in command of his material than here.

Character. Apart from the Wessex Chorus, who are dealt with separately, the main characters in this book are few. Jan Coggan and Liddy are the confidants respectively of Oak and Bathsheba. Coggan's sturdy good sense and Liddy's fresh honesty are well but briefly conveyed. Even Fanny Robin is only sketched in, so that one gets merely an impression of pathos, a pretty face, and a rather empty head. Most of the scenes she has with Troy are intended to throw a cold light on *his* character. In one scene she has been calling up to his window in the barracks. When she leaves 'a subdued exclamation was heard inside, "Ho—ho—Sergeant—ho—ho!"' By indicating that all the time he was giving curt, cruel answers to Fanny's pitiful questions, he was in bed with some slut casually picked up, Hardy has told us all we need to know about Troy, and his later attempts to analyse and to some extent defend Troy's character don't quite come off.

Because many of the scenes are confrontations between major characters, Hardy is able to give us simultaneous insights on these occasions into each, as he does in the dramatic meeting by night when, at the flash of a lantern, Troy, 'brilliant in brass and scarlet', is revealed to Bathsheba (who, significantly, is 'entangled' with him). Troy's smooth change in tone from 'Have I hurt you, mate?' to the flowery phrases in which he compliments Bathsheba, the rather tawdry implications of 'brass and scarlet', and the suggestion of an illusion in 'fairy transformation'—all these combine to make the incident not only exciting but also artificial and unnatural, like Troy. In the same way, there is a touch of cheap exhibitionism in Troy's sword-play demonstration, borne out by his later success as a showman and actor. Hardy mercilessly exposes Troy's essential shallowness by his actions, while his words, of course, are intended to reflect his cleverness.

Oak's actions are set in massive contrast with Troy's; his selfless labours at the fire, his saving the sheep (in spite of Bathsheba's infuriating condescension), his pursuit of the 'gipsies', and his heroic single-handed struggle to save the grain stacks from the lightning—all spring, primarily, from his devotion to the land. But though Oak thinks first of the value of the grain— '£750—in the finest form that money can bear . . . food for man and beast'—Hardy adds, 'It is possible that there was this golden legend under the utilitarian one: "I will help to my last effort the woman I have loved so dearly" '.

A similar contrast is Oak's conversation with Bathsheba just after the sword-play demonstration, when his massive forthrightness shows up Troy's facile flattery for what it was. Oak is unswervingly consistent, a splendid tribute to Hardy's powers of character drawing. Besides the constant use of words like 'faithful' and 'enduring' to describe Oak, we also get frequent pictures of him at work, where 'Fitness is the basis of all beauty'. Oak's speech, his 'outspoken honesty', fit him to perfection. Normally a man of few words, when he does break out his passionate sincerity is all the more notable in appeals like, 'Are ye not more to me than life itself?' Even here, this is not primarily a declaration of his love for Bathsheba; it is an earnest of his determination to save her from herself. Perhaps Hardy's greatest achievement is to show how completely Oak is in tune with his environment. Though 'one of the most gentle men on earth', when necessary he can act with 'mercurial dash'. In this he is contrasted with Bathsheba, who isn't at all sure of herself until the end of the book. At one moment she dismisses him in a fit of temper, at another begs him to return—'Do not desert me, Gabriel'. Bathsheba's flickering inconstancy is seen against Oak's unwavering devotion. At first, we tend to write Bathsheba off as a bird-brained flirt, but, where all the other characters are already mature and don't change much, Hardy shows us how his heroine grows up through the book. She gains in stature when she becomes mistress of the farm. But we feel it is all very much of an act, and this is revealed in her conversations with Liddy. The Valentine which Bathsheba sends Boldwood is the act of a silly child, and Hardy sums up her character in a nutshell with this comment on the event: 'So very idly and unreflectingly was this deed done. Of love as a spectacle Bathsheba had a fair knowledge; but of love subjectively she knew nothing.' On the other hand, Bathsheba is really sorry for what she has done to Boldwood, and though her reactions may tell us to beware of confusing pity with love, her whole relationship with him points to her warmheartedness and genuine remorse. Hardy stresses her generosity, too—something he thought vital—in showing her to acknowledge her mistakes, as when she says: 'Oh Gabriel, you are kinder than I deserve', which is certainly true. Yet she marries Troy, torn 'between jealousy and distraction', though she went to meet him with the intention of throwing him over. It is amazing how well Hardy succeeds in making this bundle of inconsistencies into a charming woman—something he achieves largely by the skill with which he exposes the essential goodness that often lies buried beneath layers of frivolity and thoughtlessness. When disaster strikes her, Bathsheba bears up heroically, and the scene where the children sing 'Lead, kindly light', with its significant line, 'Pride ruled my will', and Hardy says she would 'give anything in the world to be, as those children were, unconcerned at the meaning of their words, because too innocent to feel the necessity for any such expression', is one of the most moving and revealing in the book. She still has a little of her old spirit left, enough to be irritated at Oak's 'neglect' of her. But the scene where she agrees to marry him is full of a quiet charm which owes much to her new-found maturity.

As to Boldwood, it need only be said here that Hardy makes him contrast with Troy in every particular. Where Troy is a hollow man with a bright deceptive surface, Boldwood, outwardly unattractive, is volcanic underneath, and Hardy pictures him with bold, sweeping strokes.

The Wessex Chorus. The chapters in which the Chorus is concerned challenge comparison with Shakespeare's famous Cotswold pictures in *Henry IV*. Perhaps most remarkable is the way Hardy grips our interest in these often lengthy scenes where virtually nothing happens. The settings are well done, of course, and the detail in particular brilliantly selective. Examples are, 'the gigantic cider-mug aptly called a "God-forgive-me"' (because the drinker feels ashamed of himself when he sees its bottom after emptying it), and the bacon which Oak is not 'to chaw quite close' because ' 'tis rather gritty', though it is 'clane dirt'. Similarly the *occasions* of the talk often add interest to the book. When Cain Ball, who has just returned from Bath, tells us how he saw Bathsheba and Troy there, his rambling digressions are delightful to us and fascinating to the Chorus. Oak, however, has to suffer on the rack of Cain's gawking recollections of 'great glass windows to the shops' and 'old wooden trees in the country round'. Yet in the same scene Matthew Moon, simple as he is, can say something really perceptive about Bathsheba and Troy: 'She'll wish her cake dough if so be she's ever intimate with that man', thus voicing the feeling of the whole group.

Each member of the Chorus, however, is sharply individualised by Hardy's vivid thumbnail sketches. The maltster's age is conveyed in this fine image: 'His frosty white hair and beard [overgrew] his gnarled figure like the grey moss and lichen upon a leafless apple-tree', suggesting Father Time himself; and Laban Tall is described as 'having no individuality worth mentioning, (he) was known as Susan Tall's husband'. But it is of course primarily the *quality* of the talk—slow, even ponderous at times, repetitive, yet immensely varied, rich, racy and inventive —that draws our attention like a magnet. Yet Hardy never pokes fun at his rustics: rather he seems to suggest that their freer speech and their undisguised pleasure in what they say is an enviable quality, as indeed it is. There is a splendid rhythm, and a relish for a thing well said in Jan Coggan's tribute: 'And so you see 'twas beautiful ale, and I wished to value his kindness as much as I could, and not to be so ill-mannered as only to drink a thimbleful, which would have been insulting the man's generosity'—and he rises to a delightful climax: 'Ah, 'twould slip down sweet! Happy times! heavenly times!' Coggan also tells the tale of how Poorgrass answered the owl who said 'whoo' in superb deadpan fashion; and Henery Fray's comment on Andrew Randle's stammer is nicely poised between irony and unintentional humour: 'The only time he ever did speak plain, he said his soul was his own, and other iniquities, to the Squire'. Coggan's tribute to Parson Thirdly is delightfully sly: 'He's a generous man; he's found me in tracts for years, and I've consumed a good many in the course of a long and shady life'. It is perhaps their 'oriental indifference to the flight of time' which makes their talk itself seem timeless. But at the bottom of it all is Hardy's genius. For the secret is that he does not simply record, but selects, adapts and varies, so as to make out of everyday speech something as enduring as rock.

Background. The background in this book is as integral a part of it as is the canvas of an oil painting. The narrative marks time with the farming year, and every incident, however small, is set against the landscape. Thus where and when it happened become almost as important as how and why. Oak is perhaps the most closely linked with his environment; the various signs of the impending storm are 'a direct message from the Great Mother' to him; even the 'large toad humbly travelling across the road' tells him something. Troy, on the other hand, is out of place, having no feeling of duty to the land at all. Though Boldwood's neglect of the farm stresses his tragic plight, it is still a mark of weakness in him, whereas Bathsheba is able to overcome her pique and beg Oak's help to save her poisoned sheep. In a way then, all the main characters are judged by their devotion to the land. Since nearly all the dramatic incidents stem from natural phenomena, Hardy can avoid the coincidences he often employs rather woodenly elsewhere. As always, weather and landscape are vividly described, often by original images. Leaves in the ditch don't just rustle, they 'simmer and boil'; the wind doesn't spin them, 'a tongue of air occasionally ferrets out a few'. The stars don't simply shine, each is differentiated: 'The kingly brilliancy of Sirius pierced the eye with a steely glitter . . . Capella was yellow . . . Betelgueux shone with a fiery red.'

There are brilliant touches throughout the book. When Oak meets Liddy, and in lending her money, touches her wrist: 'He . . . felt the same quick hard beat [as] in the femoral artery of his lambs when overdriven'. This is a particularly striking instance of Hardy using Nature to throw light on human nature, and the weather or the scenery also often mirror the character's emotions. To Oak, after his sheep had been destroyed, 'the pool glittered like a dead man's eye': to Boldwood, as he happily goes to meet Bathsheba, 'the ground was melodious with ripples, and the sky with larks'.

Perhaps the finest examples of Hardy's use of background are the chapters on the great storm, which is itself splendidly described, with a wealth of detail. But the real purpose of this scene is not to describe a storm but to show how Oak and Bathsheba fall finally in love, and this though not a word of love is uttered from start to finish. For in the ordeal by terror neither flinches, but both labour fearlessly and selflessly to save the grain. In this community of effort each sees the other stripped of pretension down to the bare bones of self. It is Hardy's supreme achievement in this novel to give us a similar wordless impression in many other places where men and women, and the landscape, act upon one another.

Sense of the past. In his Preface Hardy says that 'for the presentation of legend, folk-lore, close inter-social relations, and eccentric individualities . . . the indispensable conditions . . . are attachment to the soil of one particular spot by generation after generation'. The whole of this book is *about* that attachment, about one of those spots, and it is informed throughout by mingled love and grief for a lost way of life, which is, however, treated as if it were still present. Accordingly there isn't much direct reference to the past in it, but there is one passage of a sustained magnificence Hardy nowhere else has equalled. It is the description of the vast barn where the sheep-shearing takes place. Not to quote the whole of this is almost unforgivable; it is Hardy's greatest tribute as architect, historian and poet to all the craftsmen and labourers of past ages. Hardy first stresses the size of the barn, its splendid craftsmanship and its antiquity:

> The vast porches at the sides, lofty enough to admit a waggon laden to its highest with corn on the sheaf, were spanned by heavy-pointed arches of stone, broadly and boldly cut, whose very simplicity was the origin of a grandeur not apparent in erections where more ornament has been attempted. The dusky, filmed, chestnut roof, braced and tied in by huge collars, curves and diagonals was far nobler in design, because more wealthy in material, than nine-tenths of those in our modern churches.
>
> 22

After this tribute to the men who made the barn, Hardy goes on to speak of its fitness for its purpose, which 'was the same with that to which it was still applied'. He rises to a splendid climax:

> The lanceolate windows, the time-eaten arch-stones and chamfers . . . the misty chestnut work of the rafters, referred to no exploded fortifying art or worn-out religious creed. The defence and salvation of the body by daily bread is still a study, a religion, and a desire.

This may be heretical, but it is Hardy's most profound belief, and the whole book is summed up in that last sentence. Samuel Palmer was possessed by exactly the same sense of beauty and fitness. A long look at his picture (see illustrations) will tell us much about the spirit of Hardy's book. But there is one more sentence to be quoted:

> Here the shearers knelt, the sun slanting in upon their bleached shirts, tanned arms, and the polished shears they flourished, causing

them to bristle with a thousand rays strong enough to blind a weak-eyed man.

How can we account for this heraldic sunburst which invests these very ordinary Wessex peasants with such magnificence? Perhaps by realising that Hardy saw in their unending labour the true glory of life, for 'the barn was natural to the shearers, and the shearers were in harmony with the barn'. *Far From the Madding Crowd* is Hardy's tribute to them both. It is an immortal garland.

'TESS OF THE D'URBERVILLES'

Hardy was once asked, 'Which of your novels is your favourite?' He thought for a moment and replied, simply, 'Tess'. When it was published it was hailed as 'a high-water mark of Late Victorian Fiction'. A best-seller, it was printed four times in four months, and if any reasonably well-read person were asked to name the dozen greatest English novels, it is long odds that *Tess* would figure in the list. The praise was not universal, however: Tess was a 'fallen woman', seduced by Alec d'Urberville quite early in the book, yet Hardy had the effrontery to call her 'pure' on the title-page. It was not that 'fallen women' did not exist, of course: prostitutes swarmed the London streets, and the reporting of divorce cases in the papers of the day would make the average modern reader's hair stand on end. It was even possible for editors to write about the 'sorrowful sisterhood' in terms of mild regret, and to approve of Mr. Gladstone's taking them home for tea and conversion. But Hardy had gone further; he had sailed in to attack the iron convention that, in assessing a woman's character, virginity outweighed all other considerations. What Christ had said to the woman taken in adultery and about to be stoned: 'Let him who is without sin among you cast the first stone', Hardy in effect said to his readers, and a good few responded by letting fly at him. In writing *Tess of the D'Urbervilles* Hardy, like Swift, was 'lacerated with fierce indignation', and the result is a noble and tragic book informed by a rage of pity not for Tess alone, but for all mankind. Nevertheless it isn't because it's an uncommonly eloquent sermon that we read *Tess*, but because it is a great novel and we can't put it down.

Plot and construction. The plot of *Tess of the D'Urbervilles* is simply a record of things happening to Tess, and almost the whole sequence of events is seen through her eyes, so that she dominates the story far more than any other single character in a Wessex novel. The structure is simply a see-saw, with Tess balanced in the middle; on one side what Hardy calls 'the invincible instinct towards self-delight' and on the other 'the tragedy of the worthy compassed by the inevitable' (a phrase Hardy wrote in his journal not long after completing *Tess*). The book is further tied together by a whole series of antitheses between pain and pleasure, comedy and tragedy, 'natural' love and 'unnatural' convention, over-fastidiousness and extreme coarseness, so that the zigzag of the plot is emphasised by these contrasts. Instead of the action's being forwarded simply by confrontations of the main characters, there is another force at work which we can only call destiny or fate. This force acts upon all characters, but especially upon Tess, so that intentions are continually frustrated by an unexpected turn of events, of which the failure by Angel Clare to discover Tess's written confession before their marriage (it had slipped under his door-mat) is typical. We can accept this as the kind of thing that does happen, but it must be admitted that some of Hardy's surprise-packets aren't particularly convincing: Alec d'Urberville's sudden appearance at Marlott in a smock-frock, for example, takes a good deal of swallowing from so natty a dresser.

On the whole, however, Hardy keeps an even balance between what is and what is not plausible so far as incidents are concerned. Indeed it is precisely because he constantly manages to show us vistas of possible delight opening out in front of Tess, opportunities for her to satisfy 'the appetite for joy that pervades all creation', that her repeated failure to achieve the smallest measure of lasting happiness until the very last phase of the book is so affecting. For this isn't just the record of a 68-round contest between Tess and the President of the Immortals (Hardy's ironic title for Fate, used in the final sentence) with every round won on points by the latter, and the execution of Tess for the knock-out: Tess fights back to the last, and her victories, ephemeral as they are, stand for the indomitability of the human spirit. She is Everywoman; in learning about her we learn about ourselves, and this fact, more than anything else, makes *Tess* the great novel it is. It is worth remarking here, perhaps, that Hardy opens *Tess* very skilfully, rapidly introducing all the major characters and setting the pattern of events in motion in only a few chapters—a great improvement structurally over, say, *The Return of the Native*. Indeed he maintains a pretty brisk pace all through the novel, and, though some have objected that the last section is taken at too much of a gallop, there's little doubt that this book is the best put together of any of the Wessex novels.

Thought. In places, as even Hardy's most devoted readers must admit, *Tess* shows signs of Hardy suffering from a 'rush of brains to the head'. It is at times overloaded with ideas, most of which were worth airing, and nearly all of which bear on the plot in one way or another; but Hardy's thrifty use of material on the Dorset Labourer (from an essay he had previously published) results in the insertion of rather heavy lumps of social reform, and it is a pity he was obliged to hedge Tess's seduction by Alec d'Urberville with so dense a thicket of excuses, in what one assumes was an effort to placate Mrs. Grundy. For example, Tess is between 'archness and real dismay' not long before the seduction, and, we are told, 'blinded by ardent manners, she had been stirred to confused surrender'—yet later on it is strongly hinted that Tess was in fact raped by d'Urberville. This, if true, would have altered the whole trend of the novel, which is that, as Mrs. Durbeyfield says, ' 'Tis Nater after all'.

For one of Hardy's main lines of thought is not only that it was Tess's destiny to fall a victim to Alec d'Urberville but that her destiny was in part a product of her upbringing. What with Mrs. Durbeyfield's sleazy good humour and 'Sir' John's beery indolence, their superstitions, ambitions and the flock of younger children, the dice are loaded against Tess from the start, as (Hardy implies) they are loaded against all the rural poor, who have no longer even the traditional supports of village life to lean on, because they are pushed by economic pressure into a desperate mobility. 'Wasted for want of chances'—Tess's remark—does not apply to her only.

Into this main thread of 'It was to be', which thickens as the end of the book approaches, Hardy weaves another. This is the contrast, already strongly marked in *Jude* and other novels, between Illusion and Reality. Hardy is very much concerned to stress this in *Tess*; and his attack on the 'arbitrary laws of society', which make Tess impure—though 'nothing in Nature condemns her'—is an aspect of that preference for the ideal over the real (introduced as early as page 3) which he thought one of the most widespread and dangerous of human prejudices. It is, for instance, significant that Angel meets Tess in the summer fog which gives her 'a strange and ethereal beauty'. When the mist vanishes she becomes real again, but Angel continues to see her as an.ideal. In the same way Tess, roving in the woods she loves, sees 'a cloud of moral hobgoblins by which she was terrified without reason. Yet it was they who were out of harmony with her environment, not she'. It is the tragic flaw in Tess's character that she can't accept what's happened—as her parents and friends could do—and put it out of her mind, because she deludes herself, sees herself as 'guilt intruding upon innocence'. In fact, 'to all humankind besides herself, Tess is only a passing thought. But for the world's opinion, those experiences would have been simply a liberal education.' Yet Tess herself meditates on Angel to this effect: ' "She who you love is not my real self, but one in my image; the one I might have been." '

Hardy pursues this idea through many ramifications. Perhaps the most important single scene is the one where ideal and real collide head-on when Tess and Angel exchange confessions. Tess forgives, almost ignores, Angel's admission of his own guilt. It doesn't change her conception of him at all. But there follows this harrowing exchange:

' "I thought, Angel, that you loved me—me, my very self! If it is I you do love, O how can it be that you look and speak so? It frightens me! Having begun to love you, I love you for ever—in all changes, in all disgraces, because you are yourself. I ask no more. Then how can you, O my own husband, stop loving me?" He answers her, "I repeat, the woman I have been loving is not you." "But who?" "Another woman in your shape." '

XXXV

It is indeed such piercing insights into the substance of the human heart as this which really constitute the 'thought' of *Tess*. On the other hand, the dreadful irony whereby love destroys itself by its own intensity (it is because Angel and Tess genuinely love each other that they confess), and the sublime pathos of Tess's final brief happiness—these, in the end, cannot be separated from the whole experience of the novel. Hardy's ideas, however, sometimes jut out awkwardly from the fabric of the book: every now and then he jumps briskly on to his soap-box and harangues us. It is only fair to give examples of this weakness —generally a failure in cohesion, since the ideas are not so much inappropriate as imperfectly worked in. When Hardy is determined to preach, he will cobble his sermon on anyhow, as in this comment on Tess's ecstatic singing of the Benedicite after her arrival in the Vale of the Great Dairies: 'And probably the half-unconscious rhapsody was a Fetichistic utterance in a Mono-theistic setting'—a stodgy addition which doesn't clarify the issue.

There are times, too, when Hardy's introduction of troops of philosophers and gobbets of their philosophies makes the book unbalanced, though on the other hand the comparison of Angel with Shelley, the 'beautiful but ineffectual angel' (Arnold's phrase, which was probably in Hardy's mind) is illuminating. But what is detachable is in the end of little importance. Where Hardy's powerful intellect and all-embracing sympathy are working in harmony with his literary instincts, his thought irradiates the entire fabric of the novel. In short, where the thought is of crucial importance, it both arises out of and gives rise to the structure. Hardy's thought is indisseverable from his presentation of Tess herself: she *is*, in her entirety, his thought; and what she stands for, in terms of patience and long-suffering, human weakness and strength, ecstasy and agony, is what the

novel is *saying*, what Hardy wants us to 'feel upon our pulses'.
Style. Tess isn't free from stylistic blemishes. When Hardy
writes: 'But the circumstance was sufficient to lead him to select
Tess in preference to the other pretty milkmaids when he wished
to contemplate contiguous womankind', what he really means is:
'Because of this Angel preferred to look at Tess'. Yet the same
paragraph begins: 'And then he seemed to discern in her something that was familiar, something which carried him back into a
joyous and unforeseeing past', which perfectly conveys Angel's
state of mind, and in the phrase 'joyous and unforeseeing past',
hits off a condition which Hardy himself knew well and every
reader recognises. It is in the dialogue that Hardy is most ham-
fisted: the itch to kick Angel is often exacerbated by the monstrous things Hardy makes him say. As usual then, Hardy wavers
from good to bad: there are moments when his control sags
badly. Still, such moments are few. *Tess* contains fewer of the
flaws we have seen occurring in his prose than almost any other
of the Wessex novels. There is little dialect, but that little is
marvellous. Only Hardy could have written Izzy's phrase on
Tess's devotion to her lost Angel: 'Her mind can no more be
heaved from that one place where it do bide than a stooded
waggon from the hole he's in.' Similarly not only is there
humour and sharp observation in this description of the drunken
revellers whom Tess accompanies on her way home to Marlott,
but Hardy has also shown us how they felt in this sentence: 'They
were as sublime as the moon and stars above them, and the moon
and stars were as ardent as they.'

In contrast to this, Hardy can show us Tess (equally unaware
of the effect she is making) as beautiful, when she is herself
christening her child, 'a thick cable of twisted dark hair hanging
straight down her back to her waist; her high enthusiasm having a
transfiguring effect upon the face which had been her undoing,
showing it as a thing of immaculate beauty, with a touch of
dignity that was almost regal'. He can also show her physical
attractiveness in one sentence: 'Having been lying down in her
clothes she was as warm as a sunned cat'.

Probably the best example of Hardy's flexible descriptive style occurs where he is showing us Tess as she listens to Angel playing the harp. First Tess walks through the uncultivated garden, 'damp and rank with juicy grass which sent up mists of pollen at a touch. . . . She went stealthily as a cat through this profusion of growth, gathering cuckoo-spittal on her skirts, cracking snails that were underfoot, staining her hands with thistle-milk and slug-slime, and rubbing off upon her naked arms sticky blights.' Not only is this precise, unpleasantly so indeed; it also suggests the real purity of Tess, whom these things, 'rank and gross in nature', only *appear* to defile; just as the opinion of society sticks to her reputation like the 'slug-slime' and 'sticky blights'. Now, as she listens to the music, the physical aspect is transposed into the spiritual, and by a brilliant change of emphasis the garden becomes beautiful: 'the floating pollen seemed to be his notes made visible, and the dampness of the garden the weeping of the garden's sensibility'. Thus we are enabled to see as Tess sees, to feel her emotions, so powerful and so misleading, and to enter into her world. This is subtle and powerful writing, operating always at two levels of meaning, and although Hardy does give many straightforward descriptions of landscape and weather similar to those in his other books, it is perhaps this 'density', this capacity to produce layers of implication under the surface of plain description, which marks out *Tess* as the summit of Hardy's prose style.

As a final instance, consider this beautiful evocation of the countryside:

> Or perhaps the summer fog was more general, and the meadows lay like a white sea, out of which the scattered trees rose like dangerous rocks. Birds would soar through it into the upper radiance, and hang on the wing sunning themselves, or alight on the wet rails subdividing the mead, which now shone like glass rods.
>
> XX

This is glittering and opulent, full of a beauty which Hardy perfectly conveys, yet somehow dreamlike and not quite real. Unreality is, of course, precisely what Hardy wants to convey. 'Minute diamonds of moisture from the mist hung too upon

Tess's eyelashes, and drops upon her hair like seed pearls. When the day grew quite strong and commonplace these dried off her': the individuality of Tess, herself never quite earthly, is like the mist; the harsh light of day dissolves it, and she has to 'hold her own against the other women of the world'. It is this flexibility, this capacity to express what is rich and strange mingled with what is dull and commonplace, just as life itself is a mingled yarn, that gives Hardy's style in *Tess of the D'Urbervilles* its distinction. It is nowhere better displayed than in the last chapter but one, the tragic episode where Tess sleeps in Stonehenge, and where, as Tess herself finds a momentary peace, the landscape seems to sympathise with her plight, for 'it bore that impress of reserve, taciturnity and hesitation which is usual just before day'.

Character. There is no getting over the fact that Alec d'Urberville is one of the least convincing characters that Hardy ever drew. There are moments when he behaves sympathetically, for instance when he defends Tess from the bullying Farmer Groby: ' "Don't speak to her like that", said Alec d'Urberville, his face blackening with something that was not Christianity.' But this incident, and others like it, only serve to stress his normal woodenness, and the idea of Alec with his 'dull brain' listening to —still less accepting as a working philosophy—the snippets of materialistic theories from the *Dictionnaire Philosophique* which Tess has learnt from Angel (and which Hardy wisely refrains from quoting verbatim), is ludicrous. We can believe in Alec as a blood and thunder preacher, but not as a convert to Materialism. As for Alec's romantic vocabulary, of which 'You temptress, Tess . . . you dear damned witch of Babylon. Damnation, you are very cruel,' and 'Good God, what am I to be repelled by a mere chit like you', are fair specimens, this cannot be taken seriously at all, but since Alec's principal function in the novel is as a kind of 'formal Vice' (he once compares himself to Satan) it is not so important as it might seem that he is unlifelike. Lay figure as he is, he does well enough to symbolise the kind of temptations Tess is subjected to, though one feels that Hardy might have portrayed the 'world, the flesh and the devil' in a more credible form.

With Angel Clare, Hardy has a much larger measure of success. However, he finds one problem connected with him intractable, since in proportion as our sympathies for Tess are engaged, so must our toleration of Angel diminish, when he is cruel to her. Hardy tries very hard to keep the balance even, but his own genius and the structure of the novel (where Tess is alone at the centre of the stage for a quarter of the book) conspire against him. Angel's early appearance as a 'desultory student of something and everything' is too brief to be significant. Hardy, perhaps sensing this, tries to solidify Angel by giving us an account of his unsympathetic heredity and background. His fundamentalist father and dull dogs of brothers are well sketched in, but Angel himself is still not fully realised. I think this is because Hardy wishes to imply that Angel doesn't fully understand himself. Certainly—a 'palpitating contemplative' with a 'hard logical deposit', a 'fastidious . . . Shelleyan' who is nevertheless prepared to muddy his boots as a farmer—he is a bundle of contradictions. If we remember this, and in particular if we realise what a very strong emphasis Hardy has put upon the nature of Angel's love, which is 'ethereal to a fault, imaginative to impracticability . . . creating an ideal presence . . . that conveniently drops the defects of the real', we may be better able to sympathise with, if not to condone, his behaviour to Tess when she confesses. But in the end we, like Tess, are 'appalled by the determination revealed in the depths of this gentle being she had married—the will to subdue the grosser to the subtler emotion, the substance to the conception, the flesh to the spirit'. A reference to Shelley's famous *Ode to the West Wind* is slipped into the next sentence, which runs: 'Propensities, tendencies, habits, were as dead leaves upon the tyrannous wind of his imaginative ascendency'. This is what makes him lash Tess with his tongue, where another man might have used his fist; and because of her gentleness, his pompous and scathing remarks, '. . . uncomprehending peasant woman . . . belated seedling of an effete aristocracy', cut all the deeper, stirring us to a loathing of Angel but equally to a rage of pity for Tess herself, who, it should be remembered, is not faultless.

For this is the essence of Hardy's genius in creating Tess. He makes her a kind of saint and martyr, but a flawed saint, not a wax effigy of Virtue. He describes Tess as one who 'sought not her own, thought no evil . . . and might have been Apostolic Charity herself'. Yet with withering irony she is made a martyr to religion, the religion of convention, to which Angel for all his free thinking is a slave.

Tess is Hardy's most masterly portrait of a woman, and so lovingly does he depict her, in so many different situations and from so many aspects, that only a few can be mentioned here. Her early freedom and independence are stressed, as is her innocence, and her delicacy of feeling which in part causes her tragedy: if she had been ready to echo her mother's superstitious acceptance she might have been content, if not happy. But Tess is proud; she will never beg either money or sympathy; and thus her final broken hopelessness and yielding to Alec d'Urberville are made more poignant. The characters who surround her—her father and mother and the dairymaids at Talbothays—all recognise in her someone of finer, and hence more fragile, clay than themselves. Her philosophy is perhaps a bit unconvincing. Hardy doesn't really show us how she acquired it, but her dignity and fiery temper (inherited from the d'Urber-villes) are made clear when she first rebuffs Alec. Her beauty, her 'flowerlike mouth and large tender eyes', is equally in character, since she will never *use* it to help herself. Hardy points out that there is a vein of 'recklessness' in her as well. She is then, complex, yet in all the long heart-rending scenes which follow the con-fession, Hardy never puts a foot wrong with Tess. Her farewell to Angel is only: ' "I agree to the conditions, Angel; because you know best what my punishment ought to be; only—only—don't make it more than I can bear!" ' It has been thought that here and elsewhere she is *too* long-suffering, but we must remem-ber that immediately afterwards Hardy says, 'Pride too entered into her submission'. Indeed, while she keeps this pride, and this humility, she remains Tess, essentially untouchable by Fate. In all the book there is nothing more moving than the scene where Tess puts the tormented game-birds out of their misery and says, 'Poor darlings—to suppose myself the most miserable being on earth in the sight o' such misery as yours! And not a twinge of bodily pain about me! I be not mangled, and be not bleeding, and I have two hands to feed and clothe me'. This is the 'impulse of a soul who could feel for kindred sufferers as much for herself', and this remains our final impression of her when she says, as she wakes up at Stonehenge, ' "This happiness could not have lasted. It was too much. I have had enough; and now I shall not live for you to despise me!" She stood up, shook herself, and went forward, neither of the men having moved. "I am ready", she said quietly.' She is happy with the little happiness she has at last snatched; we are anguished at her having had so little. No wonder Hardy was betrayed into saying, 'Her speech . . . will never be forgotten by those who knew her'. It seems that Tess had become real to him. She is certainly more real to us than many people whom we know.

Wessex Chorus, sense of the past, and background. There is, perhaps regrettably, no Wessex Chorus as such in *Tess of the D'Urbervilles*, though dairyman Crick and Tess's three friends among the milkmaids are well and often amusingly drawn. Since *Tess* was a 'modern' novel, set in late 19th-century Wessex, the past enters only as an occasional means of contrast. The background, however, is put in by Hardy with as firm a hand as ever. The description of Talbothays Dairy, 'that happy green tract of land where summer had been liberal in her gifts', the bleak winter at Flintcomb Ash, the dancing at Trantridge, are all as unerringly detailed as ever. But because the background here is invariably and deliberately subordinated to Hardy's thought and portrayal of Tess—because, in fact, it *is* simply background, seldom as elsewhere taking on a function of its own, I have not dealt with it here in detail. It is easy enough to discover it, but it would be unwise to extract it, I think. One cannot read *Tess of the D'Urbervilles* for its incidental felicities: the novel stands or falls by its central theme. If that is not powerful enough to hold the reader's attention, he had better stick to strip cartoons.

5

Note on 'The Dynasts' and the Short Stories

The Dynasts is unique; you cannot compare it with anything else in Literature. It is a representation in dramatic form (though not intended to be staged—it would take a whole day, I should think) of the Napoleonic Wars seen from as many different viewpoints as possible—those of Nelson, the Wessex labourer, Pitt, George III, the ordinary sailor and soldier and Napoleon himself among them—and symbolising the human predicament, as Hardy saw it, at all times. The whole vast panorama (which is described in a mixture of prose and blank verse and contains intermittent songs) is presided over by a Chorus of Spirits (representing the Years, the Pities and so on) who observe, record and comment on events, though the ultimate control lies with some far more vague power, not directly represented, called the Immanent Will. To read *The Dynasts* is to take a trip in a vast, unwieldy literary pantechnicon, crammed full of genius, high talent, fustian and codswallop, confronting us, as it alternatively roars and lurches along, now with the lumber, now with the magnificent achievement, of a great writer's mind. No one will readily set it aside if he has read on to reach one of the best passages, but no one is likely to go far if he is determined to be pernickety. It is a failure perhaps, but a noble and commanding failure beside which many successes look trivial.

Hardy wrote over forty short stories. (See Reading List for the volumes containing them.) Many were written to order and against time for magazines, and I feel that Hardy's full attention wasn't often engaged on them. Besides, the fact is that he was by inclination and choice a discursive writer, not disposed to accept the strait-jacket of so many thousand words. His full-dress 'tales' are less effective than his sketches, where an incident dictates its own shape. His short vignettes can be most effective. Those who wish to sample Hardy's short stories should try *The Three Strangers* for humour and ingenuity, *The Withered Arm* and *The Fiddler of the Reels* for macabre fantasy, and *The Distracted Preacher* for romance and satirical comedy. Wing writes enthusiastically about the short stories in his *Hardy*, but I can't go all the way with him. As against Maupassant, or such modern masters of the form as H. E. Bates, Hardy's work in this genre is too encumbered with plot and incident to make the impact its imaginative fertility deserves.

Reading List

BIOGRAPHY

F. E. Hardy: *The Life of Thomas Hardy* (Reprint House Int'l, New York, 1928), really an autobiography, and quite indispensible: this may be supplemented by C. J. Weber: *Hardy of Wessex* (Columbia Univ. Press, New York, 1965), E. Hardy: *Thomas Hardy* (Russell & Russell, New York, 1969), both lively and scholarly; and Edmund Blunden: *Thomas Hardy* (St. Martin's Press, New York, 1942), brief but acute. L. Deacon and T. Coleman: *Providence and Thomas Hardy* (Humanities Press, Inc., New York) tells us all that is known and a good deal that is not *known* about the Tryphena Sparks affair. E. L. Hardy: *Some Recollections* (Oxford Univ. Press, New York, 1965) is also of interest.

TEXTS

Prose works all available from Modern Library (New York), and—major novels and *Selected Short Stories* only—St. Martin's Press (New York).
Collected Poems; G. M. Young: *Selected Poems*; J. Wain: *Selected Shorter Poems*, PB; *The Dynasts*, edited J. Wain, are also available from St. Martin's Press (New York).
Thomas Hardy: Personal Writings, edited H. Orel (Univ. Press of Kansas, Lawrence, Kans.). Reprints many articles personal and critical which have long been out of print.

CRITICISMS

The following books are not too specialised for the general reader to profit from them.

I. Howe: *Thomas Hardy* (Macmillan, New York, 1967).

L. Johnson: *The Art of Thomas Hardy* (Haskell House Publishers, Ltd., New York, 1969). Early but still valuable on novels.

H. C. Duffin: *Thomas Hardy* (Barnes & Noble, New York, 1962). Good on novels.

D. Brown: *Thomas Hardy* (Barnes & Noble, New York, 1961). First-class analyses of poems.

A. J. Guerard: *Thomas Hardy:* A Critical Study (New Directions, New York, 1964). Very full. Perceptive. Occasionally over-does the psychological approach.

G. Wing: *Hardy* (Barnes & Noble, New York, 1966). Brief, but especially good on the short stories.

A. J. Guerard (Editor): *Hardy: A Collection of Critical Views* (Prentice-Hall, Inc., Englewood Cliffs, N.J.). Collection of essays. W. H. Auden's is particularly good.

Note: There is no good book on the poetry alone though Hynes: *Pattern of Hardy's Poetry* (Univ. of North Carolina Press, Chapel Hill, N.C.) is an interesting viewpoint.

D. H. Lawrence's long essay in *Phoenix* (Viking Press, New York) is fascinating but, as he admitted, perverse.

Dr. Leavis stands for the opposition in *New Bearings in English Poetry* (Univ. of Michigan Press, Ann Arbor, Mich., 1960) and *The Great Tradition* (New York Univ. Press, New York, 1963).

Acknowledgements

The author and publishers are indebted to the Trustees of the Hardy Estate, The Macmillan Company of Canada Ltd. and Macmillan & Co. Ltd. for permission to quote from Thomas Hardy's Works. Extracts from *I am the One, Lying Awake* and *Our Old Friend Dualism* are reprinted with permission of The Macmillan Company from *Collected Poems* by Thomas Hardy (© 1928 by Florence E. Hardy and Sydney E. Cockerell, renewed 1956 by Lloyd's Bank Ltd.) and extracts from *At Wynyard's Gap, A Philosophical Fantasy, A Night of Questionings, Snow in the Suburbs* and *The Later Autumn* are reprinted with permission of The Macmillan Company from *Collected Poems* by Thomas Hardy (© 1925 by The Macmillan Company, renewed 1953 by Lloyd's Bank Ltd.).

The bust of Hardy by Maggie Richardson is reproduced on the cover by courtesy of the Dorset Natural History and Archaeological Society; the sketch of him by William Strang by courtesy of G. McGregor-Craig; Hardy's drawing *Her Dilemma* by courtesy of the Birmingham City Museum and Art Gallery and his sketch *Searching for the Glass* by courtesy of the Trustees of the Hardy Memorial Collection, Dorset County Museum.

Hardy sometimes divided his novels into books and chapters, sometimes into chapters only. All the quotations are from Macmillan's Pocket Edition; where a Roman numeral follows an Arabic, the second is a book number.

Index

After a Journey, 84–6
Afternoon Service at Mellstock, 52
Afterwards, 9
Ah, are you digging on my grave?, 48
Amis, K. (*Lucky Jim*), 89
An August Midnight, 55
Apology to *Late Lyrics and Earlier*, 60
Arnold, M., 35
At a Lunar Eclipse, 43
At Castle Boterel, 81–2
At Middle-Field Gate in February, 63
At Wynyard's Gap, 45
Auden, W. H., 88
Austen, J., 108

Bagehot, W., 49
Barnes, W., 56, 61
Barthelemon at Vauxhall, 43
Bates, H. E., 154
Beeny Cliff, 36, 82
Beyond the Last Lamp, 62
Blake, W., 82
Blinded Bird, The, 52
Bridenight Fire, The, 46
Browning, R., 16, 22, 54
Bunyan, J. (*Pilgrim's Progress*), 13
Burns, R., 71
By the Runic Stone, 63

Cecil, Lord David, 96
Chaucer, G., 32
Chesterton, G. K., 53
Christening, The, 47
Church Romance, A, 42
Clare, J., 37, 61
Coleridge, S. T., 32, 101
Conformers, The, 71
Convergence of the Twain, The, 55
Corporal Tullidge's Tale of Valenciennes, 46

Dark-Eyed Gentleman, The, 45
Darkling Thrush, The, 52–5
Darwin, F. (*Origin of the Species*), 16
Dawn of the Dance, The, 33
De la Mare, W., 22, 40
Dead Wessex, the Dog to the Household, 56
Desperate Remedies, 18, 27, 102
Dickens, C., 25, 90, 96, 102, 108
Division, The, 71
Donne, J., 86
Dream or No, A, 76
Drinking Song, 49
Drummer Hodge, 60
Dumas, A., 13, 96
During Wind and Rain, 82
Dynasts, The, 9, 153

Eliot, T. S., 9, 88
Emerson, R. W., 31
End of the Episode, The, 69, 72–4

Far From the Madding Crowd, 12,
    18, 28, 91–2, 93–4, 128–42
Fiddler of the Reels, The, 154
Fielding, H., 13, 90, 96
Fitzgerald, E. (Omar Khayaam), 22
Five Students, The, 64–6
Friends Beyond, 57

Gaskell, Mrs. E., 25
Genoa and the Mediterranean, 62
Gibbon, E., 56
Going, The, 76–8

Hand of Ethelberta, The, 91, 97, 102
Hardy, Mrs. F. E. (Life of Thomas
    Hardy), 10
Haunter, The, 76, 80
He Abjures Love, 74
Head above the Fog, The, 63
Her Dilemma, 62
He revisits his first school, 63
Homecoming, The, 46
Hopkins, G. M., 26
Housman, A. E., 50

I am the one, 10
I found her out there, 34, 76, 79
I look into my glass, 65
In a Eweleaze near Weatherbury, 68
I need not go,. 67
In Front of the Landscape, 35, 62
In Tenebris, 51
In the Time of the Breaking of
    Nations, 61
I say I'll seek her, 71

James, H., 96, 101
Johnson, Dr. S., 57, 66, 125
Jude the Obscure, 17, 20, 28, 56, 90,
    122–8, 130
Julie-Jane, 45

Keats, J., 32, 56, 64

Lamb, C., 101
Lament, 79–80
Laodicean, A, 92, 93, 97, 102
Later Autumn, The, 64
Lausanne—In Gibbon's Old Garden,
    56
Levelled Churchyard, The, 33
Liddell, R., 91
Life and Death at Sunrise, 64
Lying Awake, 36

Maupassant, G. de, 154
Mayor of Casterbridge, The, 90, 97,
    98–100, 103–18
Memorial Brass, The, 36
Meredith, G., 56
Midnight on the Great Western, 52
Milton, J., 49, 56
Minute before Meeting, The, 41

Nature's Questioning, 50
Night of Questioning, A, 51
Novalis, 113

One Ralph Blossom Soliloquizes, 44
On Sturminster Footbridge, 63
Orphaned Old Maid, The, 45
Our Old Friend Dualism, 49
Owen, W., 37
Oxen, The, 52

Pair of Blue Eyes, A, 90, 102

Palgrave, F. T., 31
Phantom Horsewoman, The, 87
Philosophical Fantasy, A, 49
Places, 76
Poor Man and the Lady, The, 17
Pope, A., 34, 59

Rain on a Grave, 79
Regret Not Me, 57
Return of the Native, The, 108–13
Ruined Maid, The, 46–7

Saintsbury, G., 88
Satires of Circumstance II (In Church), 48, 49
Schreckhorn, The, 34, 42, 43
Scott, Sir W., 96
Self-Unseeing, The, 12
Shakespeare, W., 32, 106
   Hamlet, 121
   Henry IV Part I, 138
   King Lear, 59, 89, 113
   Love's Labour's Lost, 30
   Othello, 113
She to Him, 1 & 3, 41
Shelley, P. B., 54, 56, 126, 150
Shut out that moon, 70
Simonides, 61
Snow in the Suburbs, 64
Souls of the Slain, The, 61
Spot, A, 68–70, 73
Steinbeck, J., 113
Stevenson, R. L., 96
Sun on the Bookcase, The, 14
Surview, 60
Swift, J., 142

Tennyson, A., 31, 32, 35
Tess of the D'Urbervilles, 95–6, 142–52
Thackeray, W. M., 124

Thomas, D., 48, 83
Thomson, J., 31
Thoughts of Phena, 68
Thoughts from Sophocles, 41, 75
To an Unborn Pauper Child, 10, 57–60
To a Pet Cat, 56
To Meet or Otherwise, 73
To My Father's Violin, 56–7
To Shakespeare, 56
Trollope, A., 89
Trumpet Major, The, 97, 98, 102–3
Two on a Tower, 102
Three Strangers, The, 154

Under the Greenwood Tree, 10, 18, 27, 89, 103–8
Under the Waterfall, 82–3

Virgil, 75
Voice, The, 83, 84

We are getting to the end, 43
Weathers, 29
Weber, C. J., 97
Webster, J., 101, 130
Well-Beloved, The (poem), 67
Well-Beloved, The (novel), 102
Wessex Heights, 62
Wet Night, A, 43
When I Set Out for Lyonesse, 18
Where They Lived, 63
Withered Arm, The, 154
Woodlanders, The, 98, 118–22
Wordsworth, W., 35, 61

Year's Awakening, The, 52
Yeats, W. B., 20, 66
Young, G. M., 34
Your Last Drive, 78